# RECLAIM YOUR
# DIGITAL GOLD

## — IT IS YOUR POWER —

## HOW YOUR PERSONAL DATA IS CHANGING BUSINESS

## WAYNE HINDS

Reclaim Your

# DIGITAL GOLD

## It Is Your Power

## How Your Personal Data Is Changing Business

The Digital Age Requires More Data To Power Society's New Engine.

# CONTENTS

In loving memory.

To Steve, my brother and friend.

Thank you for sharing in
my season of deep inspiration and transition.
But you left us far too soon.

"Mad love" my brother.

# INTRODUCTION

Data has quickly become one of the world's most valuable commodities, and we are willing to trade our personal information for convenience, entertainment, and instant gratification.

As a result of the widespread acceptance of the Internet, booming mobile device usage, and vast amounts of data, new business models have emerged to meet our every need and convenience online.

Data has become the fuel to power many businesses' goals and engines. They collect, measure, and analyze it to market to people like you and me based on our searches, behavioral habits, and purchasing patterns.

Some of these companies provide enticing behavioral and habit-changing services that will result in irreversible social change.

This book gives insight into the importance of personal data and how it is being used to shape the future of business and society.

We will explore what the future of business and society might look like, as well as practical steps you can take to reclaim and reposition your data power.

# PREFACE

Our world is changing; in fact, it has changed!

Since the arrival of the digital age, technological innovation has contributed to rapid change in every sector of society, from education to social connections, entertainment to business, and everything in between.

The widespread adoption of personal computers and mobile devices, development of email communication systems, low-cost data storage and collection, and analysis tools have paved the way for innovative businesses to enhance the ability to access and share information.

The innovation that drove the transition from print to analog to digital adoption resulted in online goods and service Apps. As a result, a few service providers have emerged as market leaders in data collection to develop habit-forming consumer Applications. Today, these few providers have collectively transformed entertainment, social interaction, and how we communicate.

Data has become one of the world's most important assets — more data has been collected and stored in the last ten years than in the previous 100. Companies use this data to conduct micromarketing, which targets your wants and needs based on your previously tracked search habits and purchasing patterns.

As a result, a new industry has emerged: Big Tech, also known as the tech giants. The leaders are Facebook, Apple, Amazon, and Google (Alphabet), to name a few, which have captured and stored the most user-generated online global data.

Big Tech online platforms offer their services (search, content sharing, social connections, entertainment, and so on) for what appears to be free, but in reality, it's in exchange for your data. Your information has become a valuable commodity. Data is being used to change the world and usher in a new era of artificial intelligence (AI) driven business models.

Data has become the new gold, and the companies that can deliver the best data will be the new oil kings of the next 50 years; according to Amazon and IBM. Some companies are in a prime position to take over this market.

Rapid Innovation. Immediate Transformation. Results Focus. Improved Efficiency. These are some phrases that best describe the last thirty years of technological advancement.

## MY JOURNEY

Throughout my life and career, I have also perceived how technology would transform our society. Allow me to take you on a journey of what I've observed over time due to technological innovation.

We used the new Commodore VIC-20 computers in my first computer class in high school. I remember how much fun it was to work on an assignment about the early stages of digital audio technology and how computer chips (microprocessors) were implanted in stereo equipment to improve the audio experience and make sound systems state-of-the-art. My research led me to believe that such equipment would become dependent on computer chips in the future.

This new and beneficial application of the chip was taking the sound and acoustic industry to a whole new level, and I was very excited with my research and presentation. I then realized this was the start of a trend — computers were here to stay, and innovative applications of computer technology would forever change the future. That's when I decided to study computer science for my postsecondary education and, eventually, as a vocation.

Interestingly, my first love was to become an artist or illustrator, creating paintings and artwork. Still, it quickly became apparent that there were limited career opportunities for artists. So, I abandoned that interest and pursued a career in computer science, as I believed it was the field of the future and that current technological trends would revolutionize our society.

I was correct.

During my school and work years, I immersed myself in this thriving industry by working on software and applications. I've seen our society change and become more reliant on computers as a result of Microsoft and Apple (who spawned the computer science industry), hardware manufacturers, and software solution development.

These forward-thinking leaders laid the foundation for new ways of creating tools and equipment to drive business improvements and efficiency.

The resulting hardware and software industries have produced innovative products and solution-based applications that have gained global acceptance by focusing on performance, efficiency, and user experience, while scaling their capacities and by targeting commercial businesses, governments, and educational sectors.

The introduction of database and reporting tools facilitated the capture and storage of large amounts of data, as well as the presentation of that data in meaningful and informative ways for analysis and action-oriented decisions.

Soon after, the "killer-app" (as it was affectionately referred to) appeared: the electronic mail (E-mail) — a transformative innovation to improve business communications at a lower cost.

The computing semiconductor and chip industry then boomed, thanks to ground-breaking high-performance chips and successful miniaturization over time. This led to the game-changing breakthrough and introduction of the Apple iPod and its "music in the pocket" as a portable device followed; the iPad and software application (App) platforms were then developed to create the new Apple eco-system.

Parallel to these advances was  the development of a high-speed highway in the sky, the Internet. Then, of course, it went mainstream and ushered in the dot-com era, which was responsible for the Internet's rapid adoption. In the last chapter, we will discuss the evolution of the internet from 1.0 to 3.0.

All of these factors contributed to where we are now in terms of innovation.

Computer hardware improvements gave way to handheld devices, and creative software development and distribution gave way to applications and platforms, and cloud computing, all while continuously improving the performance and decreasing the size of these devices.

Then came the digital revolution in which computerized processes increasingly replaced manual ones. This brought rapid transformation in every area and elevated aspects of the computer science industry to entirely new heights. Everything could now be digitized — and it was.

So, everything was in place to focus on data and leverage it as an asset. The digital transformation gave way to vast amounts of valuable data as the global population rapidly embraced technology (like personal computing, hardware storage and devices, applications, platforms, and cloud computing, and the Internet), leaving a digital footprint everywhere they went.

If that wasn't enough, the recent global (COVID-19) pandemic forced everyone online and opened up the virtual world to work, play, entertainment, and education.

So, the marriage of the digital and the semiconductor chipset is now permanent and co-dependent. In a recent interview, Intel Corporation CEO Pat Gelsinger said, "Everything is becoming digital, and everything digital runs on semiconductors." (Washington Post Live, 2022). Intel Corporation is the world's largest semiconductor chip manufacturer.

The statement made by Intel's CEO is very telling because it shows where we are and where we could go. Indeed, semiconductors are now used in almost every industry; to name a few applications, they can be found in manufacturing, stereo equipment, banking, automobiles, cell phones, mobile devices, and various health-related devices.

As you can see, you can put semiconductors in just about any product that we use daily and get the data you need to analyze, make adjustments, and make invaluable decisions. It has the potential to provide us with comfort and efficiency, as well as to save us money, improve our health, and even save lives. This proliferation of innovation is referred to as the Internet of Things (IoT), but that is a subject for another book.

I decided to write this book because all these innovations contributed to where we are now.

As I watched, our society has been transformed at such a rapid pace over the last thirty years due to the penetration and applications of computer science and technology, as well as the innovations that have resulted from them.

Today, computers and technology have impacted virtually every aspect of our lives, and the rate of change appears to be lightning fast, with adoption becoming easier and easier over time.

There is no doubt that the information age has brought about some exciting innovations that have greatly simplified our lives. However, we now live in a society where we have become completely reliant on these technological devices and on having information access at our fingertips.

We are constantly virtually connected online, anywhere and at any time. But this comes at a cost and has an impact on being human, such as becoming too lazy to think or do things for ourselves.

We have created a society in which technology makes our lives easier, and everything appears more efficient by having automation in place.

Soon, because of artificial intelligence (AI) and AI-driven innovations, businesses will be able to predict our every move and cater to our every need. We will soon be judging each other based on our online profiles and digital footprints. I enjoy seeing how technology has influenced every aspect of our lives and is responsible for changing our world by increasing efficiencies, connecting us, and causing rapid shifts in societal habits. However, I am concerned about the consequences as we become increasingly reliant on these systems and technologies.

This book gives insights into the significance of your personal data and how it is used as the new fuel for business and society's new engine. It also suggests ways for us to regain control of our data.

Remember how I stated previously that my first love and desire was to become an artist, but I chose a career path in computer science due to the limited income potential of being an artist? The game has changed even for the artist's income potential, thanks to the creation of the blockchain as a digital platform and the introduction of NFTs (Non-Fungible Tokens), which run on the blockchain and which provide a digital ownership signature for artwork. This will also be briefly discussed in this book.

This book will show you how your personal information gives you power in the digital realm! You will learn that by leaving your digital footprint and failing to take the necessary precautions to protect your data when using these online platforms and services, you are giving away your power.

It not only raises awareness of how and where data is used, but also of the impact it has on society and how its use is helping to establish new norms. We'll talk about how to keep your data safe, its monetary value and how you can monetize this new commodity. We will also look into what the future might look like, despite the fact that it is a moving target due to the rapid growth of data and technological innovation.

We will also give you Digital Gold Nuggets to take away and act on at the end of each chapter to help you reclaim your power and control over your digital gold.

I trust that you will enjoy reading this book and get some insights about your personal data as Digital Gold.

# Chapter One



n this chapter, we will go over the new gold rush that is currently taking place. And, as with the well-known historical gold rush, only those who plan ahead of time and are early adopters of this new commodity will score big. However, scoring big comes at the expense of those who generate the gold. We'll look at how we got here, the rapid growth of this new commodity, and who stands to benefit.

In today's information-based economy, data can be thought of as "digital gold." From database to Big Data (extremely large data sets), from data pools (large data repository) to data lakes (structured and unstructured data store), the data souces have exponentially evolved to terabytes (a million million bytes) and petabytes (a million gigabytes) of data. It is impossible for humans to analyze this much data without advanced technological and analytical tools such as AI.

In the past, gold was the most valuable commodity and it eventually became the global standard of exchange for commercial transactions. As a result, wherever gold was discovered, it prompted economic growth by spawning a slew of new industries and businesses that supported, serviced, and profited from gold mining and its biproducts. The gold rush of the 1900s spawned new industries as well as personal and corporate wealth. The industry is now worth trillions of dollars and continues to be one of the most valuable commodities.

The world then discovered a new type of gold: oil, which became known as "black gold." The same can be said about oil's global impact as a valuable commodity: Oil mining and exploration are big businesses in their own right, but they also support other business and economic sectors. Oil too, had spawned a new industry and increased global wealth to levels not seen since the gold rush.

As a result of the commodity of oil and its numerous biproducts, new industry sectors have emerged (such as the auto industry). Despite its dangers and environmental destructive properties, the world continues to rely on oil.

Data has emerged as the new rising commodity with the advent of the digital age, sparking a fiercely competitive race to acquire and maintain control over massive amounts of it. To put it another way, data is today's digital gold in the information economy.

Many online business platforms are available for free. But although they do not openly mention it, you will only be able to sign up for free in exchange for your data. This is explicitly stated in their Terms and Conditions and their lengthy End User License Agreement (EULA). In order to gain access to the site or platform, we are required to check the box indicating that we have read the terms and conditions and that we agree with them. This approach is the same with most online business platforms that charge a monthly subscription fee for their services.

These platforms do offer a valuable service that provides convenience and entertainment in various ways. As a result, surveillance capitalism has emerged as a new business model based on end-user data. Most online platforms, including social media and related sites, use it to generate revenue through the acquisition and exploitation of user data, for example, through advertising that is directly linked to your search patterns. This enables data to be profiled and classified based on demographics, measured habits, and interests. These systems generate technology algorithms that know more about us than we do about ourselves.

Through the use of data, the information economy has enabled Google, Facebook (currently transitioning to Meta), and Amazon to build their empires. But what is data, and why is it so important?

Data are discrete pieces of information that are typically formatted and saved with a specific purpose in mind. However, since the mid-1900s, when computer science became a recognized field, data has been most commonly referred to as information transmitted or stored electronically.

Many contemporary technological discussions now center on data. As a result, new technologies developed to manage data are constantly sparking debate about data; how we use and analyze it, and the broader consequences of its effects.

Furthermore, as innovative techniques are developed to store and harness its potential — such as Big Data and artificial intelligence — so has the term and use of the word "data" evolved.

Words like "data," "quantitative analysis," "Big Data," and "AI" may be frightening if you work in a non-technical environment. Don't be alarmed! Data doesn't have to be difficult to understand. Data is critical information that helps organizations make decisions and plan for the future more efficiently and effectively than humans can.

Here are some reasons why data is important, what you can do with it, and how it relates to business services:

## 1. Improve Our Quality of Life

Data can be used to help people live better lives. The most important reasons to use data are to improve efficiency and quality of services and processes. When used appropriately, data can be a valuable asset in enhancing one's quality of life.

## 2. Make Informed Decisions

The quantitative collection of data gives us valuable information sets to use qualitatively. Knowledge is derived from the collection and analysis of accurate information. Therefore, a lack of data can lead to inaccurate conclusions that are based on anecdotal evidence, assumptions, or a preliminary observation.

### 3. Achieve the Desired Results

Data can be used to evaluate the efficacy of a strategy. For example, when attempting to solve a problem, it is critical to collect data on how well the selected solution works and whether it needs to be improved or altered in the long run.

### 4. Look for Problems and Solutions

Businesses can use data to identify the root cause of problems. Organizations will only be able to see the connections between the activities in various locations, departments, and systems if they have access to data. Does an increase in pharmaceutical errors, for example, correlate with increased employee turnover or vacancy rates? We can develop more precise theories and more effective treatments by comparing these types of data points.

### 5. Strategy Approaches

The correct data strategy can lead to increased productivity. Organizations can better utilize scarce resources by using effective data collection and analysis. For example, let's assume that there has been an increase in severe accidents in a specific service area. This information can be scrutinized further to determine whether the increase is spread across the country or only concentrated in that single location. Instead of dealing with a system-wide issue, training, staffing, or other resources can be used to address the issue in that specific location. Organizations can also use data to determine which areas of improvement to focus on.

### 6. Record Keeping for Process Improvement

Businesses require reliable data to establish baselines, benchmarks, and targets to continue moving forward. By gathering and analyzing data, organizations will be able to set performance goals, recognize their accomplishments, and make the necessary adjustments for improvement.

## WHAT ARE COMPANIES DOING WITH YOUR DATA?

Now that we have looked at the importance of data, let's consider what companies are doing with your data.

### 1. Improving the Customer Experience

Many businesses use customer information to better understand and meet the needs of their customers. With real-time access to their ever-changing pool of data, companies can quickly pivot and adapt their digital presence, goods, or services to better fit the market by analyzing customer behavior and numerous reviews and feedback.

### 2. Turning Data into Money

Data collection companies have sprung up to profit from the sale of valuable data. There have always been a few of these companies around, but now this business sector is booming given the need for and increased value of data. Data brokers buy data and sell customer information to companies looking to target their customers more specifically or to augment or complement their data with specific information, such as demographic or industry-related data.

This new sector has grown in lockstep with the proliferation of data. Data collection and sale is not a new trend, but it becomes more valuable for advertisers when combined with multiple sources and helps to target a specific group of consumers.

Because the demand for more data is constantly increasing, having this information available is critical for advertisers. As a result, those who make money by selling information to one another and advertisers tend to use various data sources to create more comprehensive consumer and trend profiles.

## 3. Information Security

Some businesses even use customer data to protect sensitive information. Voice recognition data is used by banks, for example, to allow customers to access their financial information or to protect them from fraudsters. When a customer's account is accessed, data from call center interactions, machine learning algorithms, and tracking technologies are used to detect and flag suspicious activity.

In the 1990s, I worked for a market research firm where data was second only to human resources in terms of value. They had strict security systems in place to allow people to enter and exit the building. Employees were subjected to turnstiles and had their electronic devices scanned for unauthorized use.

### 4. Stored Indefinitely

Nowadays, it is widespread for us to enter our information into one system, digital platform, or website and then move on without thinking about it.

Also, many websites leave their footprint on our computers or devices because we permitted them to do so. This is done by accepting their cookies — bits of information about their site — so the page loads more efficiently the next time you visit.

Customers frequently save their credit card information when purchasing online or using an email service; and this data is commonly kept for an extended period. Unless you give them permission, most websites that save your information won't do much with it. On the other hand, some websites are insufficiently secure and do not encrypt their data. As a result, hackers may successfully break in. The bottom line is that you should be cautious about what you disclose on the Internet because you never know where it will lead.

## THE SOCIAL IMPLICATIONS OF DATA

Let's take a look at how data affects society as a whole and the trends it drives.

### 1. Medical Care and HealthTech

Data analytics is speeding up research; for example, DNA strings can now be decoded in minutes, allowing for faster cure development and the ability to predict disease patterns more effectively.

Data is being used in some hospital special units to keep an eye on premature and sick babies, and the techniques allow doctors to monitor every heartbeat and breath. Algorithms that can predict infections 24 hours in advance of the onset of symptoms are being developed.

The goal of HealthTech is to have enough information about each individual to provide evidence-based treatment tailored to them. People could take a more active role in their health and well-being if they had precise information like this. Scientists predict that new smart devices will be used for at home healthcare to push the envelope even further.

Consider a future in which your toothbrush, toilet, and scale can all tell you about your health in real-time. We already have such devices capable of producing the data needed and making that happen. We also have the tools to analyze and build the necessary health insights — they just need to be improved for quality and reliability and pooled together to provide a comprehensive health diagnosis for the user.

## 2. Applied Science

Data analytics has taken scientific research to another level. Big Data in the science field, for example, generates such large amounts of data that scientists determine the composition of the universe.

Data is also being used to aid space exploration. However, there can be a problem with having too much data. It is useless unless it can be processed and proven to be reliable and consistently accurate given the risks of space exploration.

One company that has produced  consistent results — who is at the forefront of space exploration now — is SpaceX, an American spacecraft manufacturer, space launch provider, and a satellite communications corporation founded by Elon Musk.They use data to send rockets to space and bring them back to earth to be re-used.

## 3. The Financial Sector

Data has also been used to affect many changes in the financial industry. In High-Frequency Trading, data algorithms are used to make trading decisions; in fact, the majority of equity trading is now algorithm-based. These tools can make buy and sell decisions in a fraction of a second by utilizing social media networks and news websites.

Data is also used to monitor financial institutions' trading activity. New regulations have been put in place internationally to ensure that all pre-trade communications data is reported so they can be analyzed by applying various rules to match the data to relevant financial transactions.

However, this is not the only thing these systems can do; they can also search for problems and help prevent rogue trading or trading errors.

## 4. Security Technology

Our world is becoming increasingly reliant on computer technology, and there is no indication that this trend will stop anytime soon. The Digital Age has a lot going for it regarding convenience and efficiency. It is, however, fraught with risks, not the least of which is the difficulty in preventing data breaches. Fighting cybercrime is becoming more difficult, but when data is combined with AI, it can be a powerful weapon — collaboration and information sharing can make it much more difficult to hack into networks.

Data analysis is primarily concerned with identifying patterns, and cybersecurity experts can track down malicious entities by following the trail of clues they leave behind. Even if a company's security system has flaws, data analysis can help them respond to an attack while it is happening, reducing or even stopping breaches. It should be noted that the tools used in Big Data can also be vulnerable. Sensors, in particular, can be hacked and used in botnet (network of private computers infected with malicious software) or for other nefarious purposes.

## 5. Reducing Energy Waste

With the world focused on climate change, lowering carbon emissions has emerged as a top priority. Using less energy each day is the most effective way to combat global warming and energy experts have known this for a long time.

Anyone who wants to reduce waste can benefit significantly from leveraging data. For example, smart meters and other sensors can help a power company determine when and where to generate and distribute energy, thus reducing waste. In addition, governments can levy taxes or provide rebates to encourage people to use less energy. Data helps to figure out how to use less energy, as customers are given more information about how much energy they use and how to save energy by changing when they use it. In addition, collaboration with energy providers can help large businesses reduce their energy consumption; especially industrial entities that use electricity extensively.

## 6. Enhancement of Human-Computer Interaction

People dislike speaking with an automated system because sometimes they do not know what to do, as extended menu options can make it difficult for users to find what they're looking for. Because of data, service providers can have faster, more accurate, and more reliable interactions with customers, making their lives easier and their service better.

Furthermore, these systems can learn over time, allowing them to assist customers more quickly while also lowering the costs of providing customer service and support. It is advantageous in several ways. First, voice recognition has dramatically improved as a result of data and machine learning (ML). Second, many self-help systems have advanced to the point where they can predict which services customers require. Computers will be able to assist people much more quickly and easily in the future, and the use of data can make this happen even faster.

The Information Age is still very much alive and well, but it is getting better all the time. It's no surprise that "Big Data" is taking center stage right now, given the rapid growth of the Internet of Things (IoT). In recent years, Big Data has had a significant impact on how we live our personal and professional lives. We will continue to see a substantial shift in how we live as technology advances.

## 7. Automobile Manufacturing Industries

The automotive industry has been using data to power its manufacturing robots for decades to improve quality, increase production, and satisfy customers.

Automobile manufacturers are now gearing up for the next big shift in the data revolution. Cars are undoubtedly the second most popular piece of technology in use today, trailing only mobile phones. Thanks to data analytics, the industry manufactures and sells more vehicles than ever, and automotive innovation in the form of self-driving and electric vehicles is transforming the world.

Because of Big Data, there is a new way to look at the automobile industry: it is now possible to design a car to meet the needs of those who desire customization. This enables auto manufacturers to show the rest of the world that they are cutting-edge; Tesla is an excellent example. Tesla, Inc. is an electric vehicle manufacturer and clean energy company co-founded and led by Elon Musk. In the coming years, data will be at the core of the automotive industry.

## 8. Recreation

Consuming media and entertainment have become a regular part of our lives, and we are very excited about trying new ways to consume content while having the freedom to watch when and where we want. Not to say we didn't have a choice before, but things have changed dramatically. There are now numerous options, and they can be streamed on a variety of devices, making them more user-friendly and available on-demand.

Big Data has aided in the accessibility and processing of real-time data of various types and in the development and success of these new entertainment sources, according to those in the media and entertainment industries.

Big Data has been making waves for a while now, but it is currently having a significant impact on the entertainment industry. Utilizing data is the only way to get a clear picture of customers' viewing habits to cater to their specific needs. For example, entertainment and streaming services companies such as Netflix can use a customer's age, location, language, and other characteristics to change their behavior and keep them interested.

## 9. Sports and Analytics

I'm a huge sports fan, and I never imagined that sports and data and analytics would go together, but that's all changed now. Nowadays, data is everywhere in sports. Sports teams are utilizing data in novel ways. Sports analytics is also a lucrative industry. For example, although sabremetrics (analytics) has been around since the 1980s, it really took off with Oakland Athletics General Manager Billy Beane in the 2000s. Billy Beane was a former baseball player who was the first person in sports history to make a roster decision based on statistical data from a player's previous performances. According to Billy Beane, a team's run total was determined solely by statistical analysis. Teams with a high on-base percentage score more runs.

The film Moneyball, directed by Bennett Miller, written by Steven Zaillian and Aaron Sorkin, and starring Brad Pitt, is about Billy Beane's baseball team (Oakland A's) and how they used sports and analytics to have a really competitive team and season.

This true story is an exciting look at how data and analytics were used to change the game and have since spread to almost every sports league.

In this film, Billy Beane decided not to acquire or invest in some of the biggest names available in free trade, which is a very common way to bolster a team's roster, but instead to rely on data and analytics to help build the roster, specifically players hitting and on-base performance analytics.

Everyone thought the team had gone insane because it had never been done before; evaluating players based on what they have done and what scouts say was the standard practice. Most baseball analysts believed it was a mediocre team at best, especially given that it had one of baseball's lowest payrolls that year. It proved to be a huge success. By using sabermetrics, they won a league-record of 20 consecutive games to win their division and advance to the playoffs. Since then, many major sports leagues have incorporated data and analytics into their evaluation of talent, performance, and game pay.

So far, we've discussed Major League Baseball's impact as trend setters through the use of sabermetrics, as well as how it has transformed the game. In addition, data and analytics have become an important part of the NHL (National Hockey League) in their use to aid in player analysis, conditioning, performance and assessment, and overall game improvement. And data is collected in all aspects of the game in the NFL (National Football League), and the league has partnered with

Amazon's AWS to leverage the power of its data through sophisticated analytics and machine learning to create new stats, improve player health and safety, and create a better experience for fans and players. They collect nearly 300 million data points per season by tracking player performance as well as every player on every play in every NFL game (Hardesty, 2022). Every sports league appears to have implemented sports analytics in everything from player strength and conditioning to player safety, thereby increasing the value of the game, sport, and entertainment value.

# Chapter Summary

In this chapter, we've looked at why data is referred to as "digital gold" and how it affects almost every aspect of society today. It has quickly become one of the world's most valuable commodity in such a short period of time, due in part to the digital revolution.

An important point to note is that the information economy has enabled Google, Facebook, and Amazon to build their empires in a relatively short period of time through the use of data and information.

Here are some noteworthy reasons why data and its applications are so important, as well as how they relate to businesses:

- It has the potential to improve our standard of living
- It assists us in making more informed decisions
- It is capable of assisting us in achieving the desired results in an efficient manner; and
- It can help identify the root cause of problems and solutions.

We've also seen that data can be stored indefinitely and how our personal information can be transformed to help improve the customer experience, generate revenue, and drive information security.

Furthermore, social implications of data in the following areas are also discussed. Medical Care and HealthTech,

Applied Science, Security Technology, Energy Waste Reduction, Human-Computer Interaction Enhancement, Automobile Manufacturing Industries, Recreation, and Sports Analytics are all fields where data has had or will have a significant impact.

We are rapidly approaching an insurmountable amount of data that will be incomprehensible and impossible to process without the assistance of AI and ML as a result of the digital revolution and the proliferation of device connectivity and online users.

## Digital Gold Nugget

- *Your data is valuable like gold. Protect it and learn how to leverage it!*

# Chapter Two

# INFORMATION IS POWER

n this chapter, we will show how digital information is the driving force behind today's digital world and how digital literacy creates gaps between groups in society. The digital society relies on information to create profit and transfer power. The long-term preservation and extensive dissemination of data are essential in today's interconnected society. It is possible to boost the power of the same information that existed in the analog world exponentially, by sharing it on digital networks.

Information in the digital world is intangible. It can, however, last indefinitely once it is recorded. This new method of exchanging knowledge creates a division between people who can and cannot use it as a resource. Information fluency is defined as the capacity to find data, translate it into information, and apply it offline.

## WHAT EXACTLY IS THIS DIGITAL DIVIDE?

The term "digital divide" refers to the disparity that exists between populations and geographical areas in terms of who has access to current information and communications technologies and who does not. The term currently incorporates the technical and financial ability to employ available technology, together with access (or a lack of access) to the Internet. But the gap that it refers to is continually widening with the advancement of technology.

When the term "digital divide" was originally used, in the latter part of the 20th century, for example, it referred to the divide between those who had access to cellphones and those who did not.

There are digital gaps between industrialized countries and developing countries, urban and rural populations, young and educated people, and older and less educated people. The gap between urban and rural areas is the single most important contributor to the digital divide. Isolation, which can have negative effects on mental health, educational hurdles in an era where more and more postsecondary education is being offered online, and a worsening of gender discrimination are some of the implications of the digital divide.

The global coronavirus pandemic has brought to light the disparities in digital coverage that exist across the globe, such as those that exist among children who are required to attend school off-site and those that exist in less affluent communities, where residents have had difficulty scheduling vaccination appointments.

## UNDERSTANDING THE DIFFERENCE BETWEEN DIGITAL AND ANALOG

The term "digital divide" refers to the disparity that exists between those who have access to reasonably priced and dependable Internet service and those who do not, as well as the knowledge and tools necessary to make full use of such Internet service.

This is a problem in many countries, particularly in rural areas, where individuals are significantly more likely to be disconnected from modern technologies than those living in cities. In addition, the split can be seen between countries and continents. And it exists between men and women: In 2020, 62 percent of the world's male population used the Internet, but only 57 percent of the world's female population did so (International Telecommunication Union (ITU), 2020). This disparity between the sexes has been gradually closing over the course of the previous decade.

Other forms of digital divides exist in addition to those that exist between developed and developing countries, rural and urban people, and men and women. These divides include the following:

**1. The Access Gap**: This is the most obvious example of the digital divide. It is a reference to the socioeconomic gaps that exist between people and the impact that these variations have on their capacity to buy the devices that are required to connect to the Internet. In developing nations, many people do not have enough access to technology or the Internet, and those who do have it often lack the knowledge and skills required to make effective use of it.

**2. The Usage Gap**: This is a reference to the differences that exist between people in terms of the levels of skills that they possess. There is a knowledge gap between younger and older people when it comes to being able to utilize the Internet effectively. The standard of education that a person has access to is another factor that plays a role in this. People who are younger and have more education typically have more skills than people who are older and have less education.

**3. The Usability Gap**: This one is a little complicated. It is a reference to the myriad of methods in which people utilize the Internet, as well as the fact that some individuals are substantially better equipped than others to derive the information they require from it.

Existing disparities in wealth and access to educational opportunities, as well as prejudice based on gender, are reflected in these skills and connectivity inequalities. The digital gap also makes these differences worse by preventing many people from accessing the information they need to improve their living circumstances and break out of the cycle of poverty in which they are trapped.

## THE DIGITAL GAP AROUND THE WORLD

For a significant amount of time, the global digital divide was interpreted as a result of the progression of economic development. It was generally believed that as nations and individuals became richer, they would buy digital gadgets and infrastructure, so bringing an end to the digital gap as a logical consequence of this trend.

Despite the fact that incomes have increased around the globe over the course of the past two decades, access to digital services continues to be limited in a significant portion of the developing world. This is often the result of insufficient funds being invested in the physical infrastructure of the Internet. Citizens may have equipment that can connect to the Internet, but they do not have a link to the World Wide Web due to a lack of or poor infrastructure. The percentage of people who have access to the Internet still varies greatly between continents: for example, 80 percent of people living in Europe had access to the Internet in 2022, whereas only 22 percent of people living in Africa had access to the Internet (World Bank Group, 2018).

These figures, on the other hand, conceal a significant amount of variance that exists among countries and regions. Even when they are developing in other areas, large countries that border oceans typically have considerably greater access to the Internet than smaller ones that do not. As a result of this, the International Telecommunication Union (ITU), which is an agency of the United Nations responsible for information and communication technologies, began compiling statistics on landlocked developing countries and small island developing states based on aggregate statistics pertaining to the developing world.

In a similar manner, even within nations that are considered to be highly developed, there are significant gaps in people's access to the Internet. Many people in the rural areas of developed countries still do not have access to the Internet, and many more of them lack the skills necessary to make the most of the Internet they do have. Age and country are not, in fact, the factors that are the most reliable indicators of the digital divide. The urban-rural split and the educational level are the two factors that are. Recent studies have shown that people who live in urban areas of the world have nearly twice the amount of Internet connectivity in their homes compared to those who live in rural areas of the world.

Some observers are concerned that rather than closing, the digital divide is widening at an alarming rate. Even among countries that are considered to be developed, it appears that some unethical corporate practices are expanding the gap: The current discussions around the neutrality of the Internet and versioning can be interpreted as issues of equitable access to the digital world.

## THE REPERCUSSIONS OF A WIDENING DIGITAL GAP

**1. Isolation combined with a lack of communication**: The COVID-19 outbreak has thrown into sharp light the sense of isolation that can soon be experienced by people who do not have access to the Internet or expertise in its use. It is possible for this to have a number of negative repercussions that occur simultaneously, including the inability to schedule appointments for immunization against the coronavirus, a reduction in individuals' employment opportunities, and an impact on their mental health.

**2. Barriers to education**: As more and more education is provided online, individuals who lack the means necessary to access the Internet (such as kids who have been limited to remote learning, just as it happened in 2020 because of the COVID-19 epidemic), risk being cut off from opportunities to enhance their abilities. As a consequence of this, children may have educational deficiencies, and adults may fail to take advantage of work possibilities or fail to acquire the fundamental skills required to make a positive contribution to their community.

**3. Exacerbating gender Inequality**: As was just mentioned, the digital divide also makes many forms of discrimination that are already present far more severe. Discrimination on the basis of gender is one of the most common forms, in certain parts of the world. If women do not have equal access to the Internet, they are unable to obtain an education or knowledge that would assist them in challenging their status (and increasing the likelihood that they will succeed in doing so).

These repercussions are likely going to become even more severe and pervasive as global dependence on digital technologies continues to grow. It is necessary for societies to confront the digital gap in an all-encompassing manner that takes into account the myriad of negative repercussions and characteristics it entails.

## WHERE DO WE STAND IN RELATION TO THE DIVIDE?

This difference manifests itself in a multitude of different ways, such as between men and women, industrialized and poor countries, urban and rural areas, and even countries that border oceans and countries that are landlocked. In every one of those scenarios, the first category is faring significantly better than the second.

In some areas, the inequality is so severe that it leads to unequal education, with some students having little or no access to equipment. Hardware, software, and support are in short supply. As a result, teachers should ensure that they are aware of their students' use of technology and the Internet. They should involve parents in their children's education and provide students with additional opportunities to use the Internet at school. They must pay attention to what works and what does not work in terms of technology use, stay current on the latest innovations, and adapt to the students' needs. They should also select an age-appropriate device to improve learning and create engaging lessons that relate to the digital technology in the classroom. Professional development, webinars, social media, peer collaboration, and a willingness to fail can also be beneficial.

However, it is not sufficient to delegate responsibility to parents and teachers; where possible, governments and institutions must lead the way in bringing technology to their country, making it available, and staying current with changes in order to avoid falling behind.

Information is power, but only those who have access to it can tap into it.

# Chapter Summary

We have seen that there is a technological imbalance known as the digital divide that exists all over the world.

The divide between those who have access to modern technology and those who do not continues to grow. As a result of the imbalance, digitalization is not occurring equally. The problem is that not all cultures have access to computers or the Internet.

We've also seen that the divide is related to gender, socioeconomic status and other demographics, as well as education. It can also be defined as a difference in the way technology is used and accessed, as well as keeping up with the most recent innovations.

Certain socioeconomic groups have fewer opportunities to access the same technologies, and as a result, the educational gap widens in schools with limited resources and support.

## Digital Gold Nugget

♦ *Be Information fluent: Don't get caught in the digital divide. Learn how to get access to, and how to use and leverage digital resources.*

# Chapter Three

# DATA COLLECTION HARVESTING

I n this chapter, we will discuss Data Mining which includes Data Harvesting and Data Collection. We will also learn why it is critical for you to understand data mining and how data is trained for AI use. Its function remains the same regardless of how it is referred to. The goal of Data Collection is to extract relevant data from existing or new data sources. On the other hand, data mining is the practice of analyzing large databases in order to generate new information.

New data is created every day all over the world. According to a 2017 Economist article, data has surpassed oil as the world's most valuable commodity (Economist, 2017). International Data Corporation (IDC) predicts that global data volume will increase from 33 zettabytes to 175 zettabytes by 2025. It is impossible to comprehend, organize, and categorize this much data without the proper tools. However, artificial intelligence (AI) and machine learning (ML) have greatly simplified data organization and categorization. To accomplish this, the AI and ML must first be linked to the appropriate data source or sources before being trained/programmed to process it.

Let's start with a look at the various data collection methods and data sources that result from data harvesting.

## HOW IS DATA COLLECTED?

The methods and data sources most commonly used for building machine learning models are summarized below:

### 1.  Traditional Data Collection Methods

Many businesses have had technology systems that process and/or collect data over time, making such data invaluable to their operations today. Some of these systems are made up of databases that contain information about products, inventory, sales, and customers, as well as transactional level data.

The retail industry has some of the most comprehensive and historical data due to the various POS (Point Of Sale) systems and manufacturer databanks. When combined with the data continuum from product manufacturer to retailer to consumer level data, this can be a powerful data lake. Any industry could claim the same; however, the manufacturing, banking, insurance, CPG (Consumer Package Goods), and automotive industries have led the way in amassing such traditional data aggregates over decades.

## 2. Free and Open Dataset Access

Open-source datasets are the most efficient and straightforward way to collect data for your machine learning model. Thousands of open-source datasets, similar to coding snippets, are available online. They are completely free, easy to find, and time-saving. Even if public datasets appear to contain an infinite amount of rich, detailed data, they may still require cleaning to meet specific requirements.

The following are some of the best places to look for free public datasets:

- Amazon
- Kaggle
- Microsoft
- Government Datasets (i.e., Stats data)
- Lionbridge AI
- Google's Datasets Search Engine
- UCI Machine Learning Repository

## 3. Scanning for Data on the Internet

Assume we want to get product information from Amazon, such as descriptions and prices. This could be accomplished through repetitive typing or copy-pasting. However, Amazon has far too many items and their prices fluctuate far too frequently for this to be feasible. This is what web scraping tools are for. They sift through a variety of Internet data. Furthermore, these tools automatically or manually search for new or updated data and store it for your convenience.

There are some excellent web scraping tools available, and some of these tools require code, while others do not. Some of them are open-source and free, while others are not.

So, we've seen some advantages to using web scraping tools, which are frequently free and don't even require coding skills to collect and update data.

People, on the other hand, are becoming increasingly concerned about data collection practices that involve gathering information about them without their knowledge or consent. To avoid legal issues with any machine learning model, make sure to collect data with permission using web scraping tools.

The following are some of the best free web scraping tools:

- ProWebScraper
- Scrapy
- ScraperAPI

## 4.  Create Synthetic Datasets

Synthetic datasets are so-called because they are generated by computer program rather than assembled from documentation of real-world events, as the name implies. They are made-up data. This is where the term "synthetic dataset" comes from. So, given the lack of real-world data, why should we even consider using synthetic data for machine learning models?

Synthetic datasets can be a particularly useful alternative when adequate real-world data cannot be obtained (or is very hard to obtain). The ability to precisely define a number of dataset features is another significant advantage of using synthetic data. These characteristics include the scope, format, and amount of noise (corruption or distortion) in the dataset.

One significant advantage of using synthetic data is that it eliminates the risk of copyright infringement or privacy issues. This is a significant advantage that should not be overlooked. This is especially intriguing if the dataset under consideration requires information that can be used to identify individuals. However, the use of synthetic data sets has a number of significant drawbacks.

First, creating synthetic data is a significant burden on the engineering side, especially if done by an individual or a small team. Second, there is a chance that bias will be introduced into the data. At this time, artificial data alone is insufficient to train advanced machine learning algorithms.

## 5. Manual Data Collection

The final option for data collection is probably the most familiar: manual data collection.

This method is very similar to the generation of synthetic datasets; the main differences are that real data is used rather than simulated data, and the data is generated manually rather than automatically.

You're probably wondering why anyone would bother generating their own data when there are so many free datasets and web scraping tools available on the Internet.

The answer is straightforward. The majority of the time, manual data generation is done through crowdsourcing.

The practice of delegating tasks to human workers in order to collect the necessary pieces of data that, when combined, form the generated dataset is referred to as "crowdsourcing." Crowdsourcing can be used to complete a wide range of tasks, from simple activities like image labelling to more involved endeavors like collaborative writing, which can involve several stages.

Amazon Mechanical Turk is by far the most popular crowdsourcing platform. Tasks are delegated to human workers on this platform, who are then compensated for successfully completing the tasks.

As you may have guessed, there are numerous disadvantages to this manual data generation. Extracting and formatting data is a very complex process that requires a substantial investment of time and money, as well as extensive technical expertise. Also, when it comes to personally identifiable information about customers, the use of data collected internally raises a number of privacy concerns, especially for businesses.

I hope you now have a better understanding of the various methods for collecting data for machine learning models.

## UNDERSTANDING THE DATA HARVESTING PROCESS

Regarding the collection and harvesting of AI data, there is one fundamental concept that must be understood. The information gathered and the analysis performed are only as accurate as the data provided. In the field of data mining and collection, the acronym GIGO is frequently used. This is a reference to the phrase "Garbage In,

Garbage Out," which essentially means that if the data provided is incorrect, the information generated as a result of its analysis will be incorrect as well.

Let us use an example to demonstrate:

Here's an interesting story about faulty data. A healthcare project was underway with the goal of lowering the cost of treating pneumonia patients. Based on their mortality risk, automated machine learning (ML) was used to sort through patient records to determine which patients should receive antibiotics at home and which should be admitted to the hospital. The ML was trained using accurate historical data from many clinics, and the resulting algorithm was dependable.

However, there was one significant exception to this rule. Asthma, one of the most dangerous illnesses that can accompany pneumonia, is almost always treated by medical professionals in intensive care, resulting in asthma patients having a significantly lower risk of death. As a result, the algorithm concluded that asthma is not as dangerous during pneumonia because there were no fatal asthmatic cases in the data. Consequently, despite having the highest risk of pneumonia complications, the algorithm recommended that asthmatics be sent home.

Data is essential for machine learning. It is the single most important factor that allows algorithms to be trained and explains why machine learning has grown in popularity in recent years. However, regardless of the actual terabytes of data available or the individual's skill level in the field of data science, if the individual is unable to make sense of the data records, a machine is nearly worthless, and it may even be dangerous.

If we want machines to behave and think like humans, we must first understand how humans learn. This will enable us to create machines that act and think like humans.

The obvious answer to the question of how humans learn is that we learn by processing data. Infants learn to walk and talk by absorbing a large amount of information (data) and processing it to recognize similarities and patterns, which may apply.

With that in mind, let's go over a simple example of how data collection works in machine learning, and then we'll use that as an opportunity to discuss the steps involved in using machine learning to draw conclusions from the data.

Assume we've been tasked with developing a method for determining whether a beverage is beer or wine. We would start with the question: "What is the difference between wine and beer?" Then we would attempt to answer that question using data. This question-answering system that we are developing is known as a "model," and the process by which we generate this model is known as "training." The goal of training is to create a dependable model that can respond to our inquiries correctly the majority of the time. However, before we can train a model, we must first collect data to use as training material. This is the point where we begin.

## IS IT A GLASS OF WINE OR A GLASS OF BEER?

The data will be obtained by observing the visual appearance of beer and wine (in this case, mugs/glasses). Data could be collected on a variety of drink elements, including everything from the amount of foam to the shape of the glass itself.

For the purposes of this explanation, we will concentrate on just two of these factors: color (expressed as a wavelength of light) and alcohol content (as a percentage). It is expected that we will be able to divide our two drink categories solely on these two characteristics. Color and alcohol will be referred to as "features" from now on.

## DATA COLLECTION

Data collection, the first serious phase of machine learning, is now underway. This stage is critical because the accuracy of the predictive model is directly proportional to the quality and quantity of data obtained. In other words, the accuracy of the predictive model will be directly determined by the data collected. In this scenario, the data we collect will include the color of each drink as well as the percentage of alcohol it contains.

| Color (let's say in hex code) | Percentage of alcohol | Label (wine or beer) |
|---|---|---|
| 610 | 5 | Beer |
| 599 | 13 | Wine |
| 693 | 14 | Wine |

Figure 1

Figure 1 shows the color, the percentage of alcohol, and whether the beverage is beer or wine. These will be the basis of our ML training data.

## DATA PREPARATION

Now that we've gathered all of our training data, it is now time to progress to the next stage of machine learning, known as "Data Preparation." During this stage, we will load our data into the appropriate setting and prepare it for use in our machine learning training.

We'll start by combining all of our data, and then we'll choose the order of appearance at random. We don't want the order in which our data is presented to influence what we discover because that isn't a factor in determining whether a beverage is beer or wine. To put it another way, when determining the characteristics of a beverage, we take neither its immediate predecessor nor its immediate successor into account.

So, let's run any relevant visualizations of your data to see if there are any important links between different factors that you can use to your advantage, as well as if there are any imbalances in the data. For example, if we collected far more data points about beer than wine, the model we train will be predisposed to guess that almost everything it sees is beer because it will be correct the majority of the time. On the other hand, the model could be exposed to an equal amount of beer and wine in the real world, which would mean that guessing "beer" would be incorrect 50% of the time.

In addition, we'll need to split the data into two parts. The first section, which will contain the majority of the data, will be used to train our model. The second section will be used to assess the performance of our trained model. Our goal is not to assess a model's ability to learn from the data that trained it, just as you would not use the same questions from your homework exercises for the exam.

There are times when the data we collect requires additional tweaking and processing. These include, but are not limited to, de-duplication, normalization, error correction, and other techniques. All of these events would occur during the data preparation process. We don't need any additional data preparation in our situation, so let's move on.

## THE MODEL SELECTION PROCEDURE

The next step in our workflow is to choose a model. Researchers and data scientists have created a wide range of models over the course of their careers. Some are best suited for image data, others for sequences (such as text or music), and still others for numerical or text-based data. We can use a tiny linear model, which is reasonably simple and should work, because we only have two features, color and alcohol content.

## TRAINING

We will now go over the training phase, which is widely regarded as the most time-consuming aspect of machine learning. During this stage of the process, we will use the data we have gathered to gradually improve our model's ability to determine whether a specific beverage is beer or wine.

This is similar to how a person feels when they first obtain their driver's license. At first, they have no idea how to use any of the pedals, knobs, or switches, let alone the proper context in which to apply any of these controls. A licensed driver, on the other hand, develops after a significant amount of experience and the correction of their errors. Furthermore, after a year of driving, they have developed a higher level of expertise. Their driving abilities have evolved as a result of driving and reacting to real-world data, which has assisted them in honing their skills.

This will be done on a smaller scale with our beverages. To be more specific, $y=m*x+b$ is the equation for a straight line, where x is the input, m is the slope of the line, b is the y-intercept, and y is the value of the line at x. The values that we can use for "training" or "adjustment" are m and b. There is no other way to influence the position of the line because the only other variables are x, which represents our input, and y, which represents our output.

There are many different m's in machine learning because there could be many different features. The sum of these m values is commonly organized into a matrix, which we will refer to as the "weights" matrix and denote with the letter W. Similarly, we will group b and refer to the resulting structure as the biases.

The training procedure starts with the selection of some random values for W and b, and then attempts to predict the output using those values. As you may have guessed, it performs quite poorly. However, we can test the accuracy of our model's forecasts by comparing them to the expected results, and then we can change the values we use for W and b so that our model produces more accurate forecasts.

This procedure is then repeated. One round of weight and bias updates is referred to as a "training step."

Let's take a closer look at what this means for our dataset in this specific scenario and context. At first glance, it appears that we've simply drawn a random line through the data. As the training progresses, it gets closer and closer to an optimal separation of wine and beer.

## EVALUATION PHASE

After the training phase is completed, it is time to evaluate the model to see if it is any good. The dataset that we previously set aside comes into play at this point in the process. The evaluation phase allows us to test our model using data that was not previously used for training. This statistic allows us to forecast how well the model will perform when applied to data that it has not yet been exposed to. This is meant to be an indication of how the model might perform in the real world.

According to the commonly used rule of thumb, a good training-evaluation split should be in the 80/20 or 70/30 range. The amount of the dataset that was initially used as the source determines a significant portion of this. If you have a large amount of data, a smaller percentage of it may be sufficient for the evaluation dataset.

## PARAMETER TUNING

Following the evaluation, we may decide to see if there is anything else we can do to improve the training. We can do this by changing the values of our parameters. When we were training, there were a few parameters that we implicitly assumed; this is an excellent opportunity to go back and evaluate those assumptions and try different values.

One such example is the number of iterations we perform on the training dataset while training. In other words, instead of "displaying" the model of the entire dataset once, we can "present" it several times. This can occasionally result in greater precision.

Another factor to consider is the "learning rate." Based on the information obtained from the previous phase of the training process, this determines how far we move the line during each step. All of these numbers influence how accurate our model can become over time, as well as how long it takes to train it.

When it comes to more complex models, the initial conditions can have a significant impact on the training process's outcome. There are differences depending on whether a model begins training with zeroes or with some distribution of values, which raises the question of which distribution should be used. These distinctions are visible, regardless of whether a model begins training with zeroes or a distribution of values.

As you can see, there is a lot to think about at this stage of the training process, and it is critical that we define what it means for a model to be "good enough." If this is not considered, one may end up adjusting the model's parameters for an extended period of time.

These parameters are commonly referred to as "hyper-parameters." Tuning or modifying these hyperparameters is still regarded as an art form and an experimental process. This procedure has a significant impact on the dataset, model, and training procedure.

We can finally put the model to work and see how it performs in real-world problems after we have completed the evaluation process and are satisfied with the training and hyperparameter settings.

To provide answers to questions, machine learning obviously relies on data. As a result, we get to answer some questions during the inference stage, also known as prediction. This is the culmination of our efforts, the point at which the benefits of machine learning become apparent.

Our model can now correctly identify whether the beverage is wine or beer based on the color and percentage of alcohol in it.

This is the most basic aspect of artificial intelligence or machine learning, and it all begins with data collection; without data, the entire structure becomes inoperable.

# Chapter Summary

As you have seen in this chapter, there are numerous methods for collecting and harvesting data. The methodology for data collection has evolved over time and technological advancements, from using free and open datasets to scraping the Internet to leveraging synthetic data generated by computer program or manually creating data.

All of these are valuable methods of gathering data for decision-making. And the simplest way to make data-driven decisions is with the assistance of AI and ML. As a result, gathering and cleaning data is critical so that it is in a structure that AI systems can handle and process efficiently. Similar to how a child learns by taking in information and acting on it only to repeat the process until they understand, data must be trained using ML processes and procedures to allow AI to determine the answer to a question or make the best decision.

We hope this has given you a better understanding of what AI data collection is and how it works.

## Digital Gold Nugget

♦ *Data is now the most valuable commodity.*
*Take a closer look at your digital footprint.*
*Understanding how your data is collected will also*
*help you understand how to protect it.*

# Chapter Four

# PRIVACY – WHAT'S THAT?

We live in a time when quintillions (a million trillion) of data bytes are produced every day and data volume doubles every two years. We now have unprecedented access to almost any information we require, but this access comes at a cost, i.e., Data for Data. For example, searching for something on the Internet appears to be harmless, but before you find the information you're looking for, you're bombarded with advertisements for the same thing. What is the mechanism that causes these advertisements to appear, and how does it all work?

## INTERNET TRACKING

Have you ever felt as if commercials were following you around? From websites to social media feeds, and possibly even as advertisements on the streaming service you use the most.

Your online activity leaves a trail of data that can be used to identify and track you. The information gathered may include your location, the type of device you're using, the advertisements you've clicked on, and even more. That's just the start.

Regardless of the privacy settings in your browser, a certain amount of information about you will always be visible to the websites that you visit. For example, as soon as you connect to the Internet, your Internet Protocol (IP) address begins broadcasting, which can be used to determine your general geographic location.

Your browser's name is also revealed, allowing websites to determine whether you're using Mozilla Firefox, Microsoft Internet Explorer, or Google Chrome. If you are using a mobile device (such as a phone, tablet, or laptop) to access the Internet, it will even display the current percentage of battery life.

Other information gleaned from your browser includes the operating system you're using, the type of central processing unit (CPU) and graphics processing unit (GPU) you're using, the screen resolution, and the browser plugins you've installed.

## YOU'RE NOT BY YOURSELF. YOU ARE BEING TRACKED. EVERYONE IS.

Tracking Internet users is almost universally accepted for web browsers and other Internet-connected devices. Websites monitor how users interact with their content to improve user experiences, and advertisers sift through our data to target us with relevant products and services, among other things.

This does not necessarily mean that you or the data collected about you are in danger. However, we should all be aware of how and why our data is collected. In the end, it is our own data.

## AN OVERVIEW OF INTERNET TRACKING

Internet tracking is the practice of monitoring and analyzing the activities of Internet users, typically with the goal of providing a more personalized experience while they browse the web.

In layman's terms, Internet tracking is the process by which websites analyze our behavior when we visit them. It's also more common than you'd think, with 79 percent of websites allegedly engaging in the practice. It is critical to note that tracking users on websites is not illegal, but it is also not widely known.

## WHY DO WEBSITES LOG OUR ACTIVITIES?

People have an irrational belief that the more they know, the more they can comprehend. However, that is, in essence, the idea behind Internet tracking: the more information websites have about us, the better they understand how to entertain us.

This can result in a faster and more convenient website browsing experience. You might even consider it useful that YouTube or Netflix is so good at recommending the show you want to binge-watch next. Or the fact that the first thing you see when you enter the Amazon website is the item you want to buy.

However, when it comes to Internet user monitoring, the user experience is not the only factor to consider. Here are some additional reasons why websites monitor us as a point of reference:

1.  Some websites may keep your user data but also sell it to advertising companies in order to target you with relevant items. This is done so that the websites can generate multiple revenue streams.

2.  Some government agencies monitor Internet users' activities in order to gather intelligence on potentially dangerous people.

3.  Companies frequently consult their website analytics, which reveal the aspects of their online properties with which customers interact most frequently, to guide the development of their content strategy and new product offerings, in order to evaluate the company's success.

4.  When it comes to improving certain aspects of a website, it is beneficial to keep a close eye on how website users interact with the site in order to identify and correct any problems.

## HOW DO WEBSITES KEEP TRACK OF US?

Websites can track us in a variety of ways, and the list has only grown longer over time. Cookies, however, remain one of the most widely used data monitoring mechanisms today. Cookies are used in some capacity by more than 40% of websites (CookiePro, 2021).

Cookies, also known as tracking cookies, store information about your interactions with a specific website. Cookies remember everything from the items in your shopping cart to the news stories you've read and even your preferred language settings.

Monitoring cookies can be compared to notetakers. Furthermore, because tracking cookies are specific to a website, you must "allow" or "reject" cookies each time you visit a new website that employs them. Third-party cookies, as the name suggests, store your user data in a separate location that may be accessible to third parties such as advertisers, as opposed to traditional tracking cookies, which keep their notes about you on the website where you visit them. Third-party cookies are most likely to blame for any advertisements that appear on your social media feed shortly after you visit an online purchasing website. Cookies from third parties are present on more than 80% of websites (CookiePro, 2021).

The following is a list of several alternative data tracking techniques that are commonly used today, as well as the types of user data that each approach collects:

1.  Web beacons, also known as web bugs or tracking beacons, record information such as the links and content that you click while visiting a website. They can also be used during the email exchange process to determine whether or not a message has been received or opened.

2.  IP addresses are assigned to all Internet-connected devices that are required for you to view a website.

When you visit a website, your IP address may be saved. They serve as identifiers for computers and devices connected to the Internet or a local area network. The abbreviation "IP" stands for "Internet Protocol," which is a set of rules that governs the structure of data transmitted over the Internet (or a local network) and is used to track your website activities. During a session, programs known as "session replay scripts" record a website visitor's behavior on a website. This activity includes the mouse movement, clicks, and scrolling of the visitor.

3.  Super-cookies, also known as favicons, are cookies that perform the same functions as regular cookies but are significantly more difficult to deny or delete.

4.  Account tracking is a type of Internet tracking that requires users' permission before monitoring their online activity while logged into a specific online account or platform. Account tracking tracks your online activity only while you are logged into that particular account or platform.

5.  Mouse tracking, also known as cursor tracking, is a type of data tracking software that monitors and records website visitors' mouse movements in order to analyze their engagement with a specific website.

6.  Browser fingerprinting is the process of creating a unique identifier for a user by piecing together information about that user's device, such as the operating system, language preferences, and time zone. This identifier is then used to track the user's entire online activity. Another method is to use canvas fingerprinting, which identifies the elements

of your HTML5 (Hypertext Markup Language version 5) canvas.

7. Cross-device tracking, also known as deterministic or probabilistic tracking, compares the websites you visit across all of your devices.

8. The click-through rate (CTR) is the number of times an online user clicks on and visits a piece of information that was suggested or advertised to them. Websites use the metric to determine either their content plans or the advertiser opportunities available.

9. Last but not least, Federated Learning of Cohorts (FLoC) is a cutting-edge Internet monitoring technology that eliminates the practice of identifying and following online users individually. Instead, they are assigned to a group of other Internet users with similar interests, and this group is collectively tracked. FLoCs made headlines in 2022 when Google announced that it would be using FLoCs to phase out its use of third-party cookies (Burgess, 2022). This was done to protect users' online privacy, which is a concern caused by website tracking.

## HOW TO AVOID BEING MONITORED WHILE ONLINE

Check that your privacy settings are the same across all of your devices. The first step in protecting your online privacy is to adjust your privacy settings on all of these common devices.

## MOBILE PHONES

1. Despite their reputation for being small enough to fit in your pocket, mobile devices come with a plethora of privacy settings options. Resetting your advertising identifiers will provide a new, unique identifier to apps that track your activity.

2. If you don't believe an App needs to know where you are, disable location tracking for that app.

3. After installing software upgrades, double-check your tracking controls to ensure that apps have not been reset to track your behavior.

4. If you do not want to be shown targeted advertisements, go to your device's privacy settings and disable ad personalization.

## LAPTOPS AND COMPUTERS

When it comes to computers, it's all about tracking cookies and deciding which ones you want to monitor you. Navigate to the privacy settings of each browser you use, then go through the list of websites to which you are currently providing access and disable access as needed. A word of caution: while websites can choose whether or not to recognize that you have disabled cookies, this method is not guaranteed to work.

## TURN ON THE "DO NOT TRACK" OPTION

You can request that your browser not track your browsing activity by using the "do not track" setting in your browser's settings. This means that your browser will no longer track your browsing habits. At the end of the day, this is just a request, and it is up to each individual website to decide whether or not to comply with it, as there is no law specifically prohibiting them from doing so.

## WEBSITES SHOULD NOT BE ALLOWED TO TRACK THEIR USERS' COOKIES

Simply click "decline" or "no" when a new website asks for your permission to enable tracking cookies. The disadvantage of this is that disabling cookie tracking may disable certain website functionality, and websites are not required to comply with your request, even if they do so voluntarily.

## UTILIZE TRACKER BLOCKERS

Tracker blockers are browser plugins that prevent online trackers from collecting information about their users.

## INSTALL AN AD BLOCKER

Ad blockers are browser plug-ins that do exactly what their name suggests: they block advertisements. Although this will not prevent your data from being collected, it will prevent websites from sending you tailored advertisements based on what they learn about you through their tracking software.

## GO INCOGNITO (UNNOTICED)

When you browse the web anonymously, your web browser does not save cookies on your computer or device. Regardless, any website you visit will be able to see your IP address because they require it in order to function. This means that your activity does not appear in your browser history, and others who use your device will not see it. Your user experience is unaffected while in Incognito mode.

## LOOK FOR HTTPS

Do you want the peace of mind that comes from knowing your data is being handled by a reliable website? Simply look for the letters "HTTPS" at the beginning of every URL you visit, as this indicates a secure connection to the website you're viewing.

## CONSIDER USING A VPN

You can make your web browsing anonymous by using a virtual private network (VPN), which encrypts your data and spoofs the location of your IP address. Consider using one to confuse people who are attempting to follow you on the Internet, which is a low-cost option.

In summary, keeping tabs on you over the Internet isn't done maliciously; however, depending on how much you value your anonymity when using the Internet, it may appear that way. All of the preceding examples demonstrate how targeted ads work. They can also be used to determine whether you want to be tracked online. However, it is recommended that you follow the majority of the above tips to protect your online privacy.

# Chapter Summary

In the digital age, the concept of privacy has all but vanished. According to the information provided in this chapter, everything is tracked online based on our search, sites we visit, and purchases we make.

Data is such a valuable commodity that we unknowingly give it away, especially when advertisers want to target their ideal client — you!

We leave a digital footprint almost everywhere we go online, and in order to access online platforms and services, we give up some of our rights to EULAs and terms and conditions.

Cookies (tracking codes) are stored on your computer or device by these service providers and platforms to remember your browsing experience and provide you with quick access to their site when you return. Advertisers, on the other hand, are sometimes tapping into some of these saved cookies to present you with their recommended purchase based on your recent search or interest.

As you can see, we live in a time when privacy is under constant assault. Although the Privacy Act and policies to protect our privacy remain in place, they are constantly challenged and exploited.

The good news is that you can regain control and protect your data by modifying your computer and device settings to enable and disable ad blocking and identifiers, tracking controls, and other privacy settings. You could also install a VPN (Virtual Private Network) to keep your information private and anonymous by encrypting it, so that it is not seen by sites you visit or advertisers.

## Digital Gold Nuggets

♦ *Reset your advertising identifiers by navigating to the privacy settings of each browser you use, then go through the list of websites to which you are currently providing access and disable it as needed.*

♦ *If you do not want to be shown targeted advertisements, go into the device's privacy settings of your device and disable ad personalization.*

♦ *Check your tracking controls again after installing software upgrades to make sure that apps have not been reset to track your behavior.*

♦ *Consider using a virtual private network (VPN) which encrypts your data.*

# Chapter Five

# THE NEW ECONOMY AND THE FUTURE

Digital technology is augmenting human capabilities, but centuries-old human practices are being disrupted. Over half of the world's population now has access to code-driven systems, which offer previously unimaginable potential as well as unprecedented risks. This chapter will look at how artificial intelligence (AI) will affect the economy and the future.

Investopedia defines artificial intelligence as the simulation of human intelligence in machines that are programmed to think like humans and mimic their actions. AI is increasingly influencing our lives and economies, and it has already had a significant impact on our society in a variety of ways. The United States and Asia are emerging as global leaders in terms of competition for its advantages.

Many people believe that AI has the potential to increase productivity and economic growth. It may improve decision-making and overall efficiency by analyzing massive amounts of data. This may lead to the introduction of new goods and services, markets, and industries, in increased customer demand and new revenue sources.

You most likely interact with AI on a daily basis without even realizing it.

Many people still associate AI with dystopian futures in science fiction, but this association is fading as AI technology advances and becomes more prevalent in our daily lives. Today, everyone is familiar with the term "artificial intelligence," and in some cases, it is present in their homes (hello Alexa, Siri, Google Home, Cortana!).

Although it is a relatively new phenomenon, the concept of artificial intelligence has been around for a long time. Alan Turing conceptualized artificial intelligence in the early 1950s by exploring the mathematical possibility of artificial intelligence, which a few years later in 1956 conference was further explored and then became accepted by researchers as an attainable reality, giving birth to the modern field of artificial intelligence. It then took several decades of hard work to make significant progress in developing an AI system and making it a technological reality. The History of Artificial Intelligence. (2017, August 28).

In the business world, AI has numerous applications, albeit in various forms. AI is already influencing nearly every business function across all industries, from the mundane to the spectacular. As AI technologies become more widely available, it becomes increasingly important to implement them in order to maintain a competitive advantage.

Here are some industries that are poised to use AI in profound ways.

## HEALTHCARE'S FUTURE WITH ARTIFICIAL INTELLIGENCE

Using artificial intelligence, nearly 86% of healthcare errors can be avoided (Deep, 2021). Patients and healthcare professionals alike will benefit from a more democratized and cost-effective healthcare system in the future, thanks to AI-powered predictive care. It is possible to use predictive analytics in conjunction with artificial intelligence to better understand how various circumstances affect a person's health (such as where they were born or what they eat or how polluted their environment is). We can anticipate AI-powered healthcare systems predicting when a person is most likely to develop a chronic condition and recommending preventative treatment to cure it before it worsens.

AI has the potential to transform medical care by allowing clinicians to better diagnose and treat their patients. Several types of research are already being conducted to develop AI-powered apps for this purpose. In the future, robots in hospitals and healthcare facilities will interact with patients, checking vital statistics and determining whether or not they need to see a doctor. This will fundamentally alter the face of healthcare as we know it. Doctors and nurses are not the only professions that will be required in the future. AI will make our clinical and healthcare data more actionable, while simplifying our lives.

## FUTURE RETAILING: ARTIFICIAL INTELLIGENCE

According to Capgemini, a global leader in consulting, technology services and digital transformation, in a 2018 report, artificial intelligence is expected to cost global retailers more than $7 billion per year by the end of the decade. However, they calculated that $7 billion investment will result in a $340 billion cost savings in business operations through automation and efficiency improvements (Capgemini, 2018).

Accenture, a leading global professional services company in information technology services and consulting, predicted in 2016 that retail sales globally would increase by 38% by the end of 2022. This increase in sales will result from AI-enabled efficiencies (Accenture, 2016).

These figures show that AI holds significant promise for retailers, with a variety of applications that can assist them in making better business decisions. AI-powered drones will soon be able to deliver packages weighing up to five pounds in as little as 30 minutes up to 15 miles (Jeff Wilke, former CEO of Amazon Worldwide Consumer, 2019). Amazon is already working on determining the safety and reliability of operations for delivering items, but there is no set timetable for commercial deployment of these drones. However, in the coming decade, it is reasonable to expect drones to deliver products in a fraction of time that deliveries take today.

Not only will there be autonomous delivery, but the future of artificial intelligence in retail will be more autonomous and personalized, with realistic scenarios such as connected dressing rooms with displays, virtual racks tailored according to data-defined personas, and a great deal of personalization based on previous history and trends, making customer choice less stressful and chaotic.

## THE FUTURE OF ARTIFICIAL INTELLIGENCE IN BUSINESS AND BANKING

Artificial intelligence will become the dominant force in a variety of industries over the next decade, thanks to AI's ability to lower costs, increase production, and improve customer experiences. Banking, Business intelligence and security are three of these industries. According to British marketing insights firm IHS Markit's analysis of artificial intelligence in the banking industry, the global business value of AI in Banking will reach $300 billion by the end of 2030 (IHS Markit, 2019). Robo Advisors will soon be commonplace in wealth management and will be game changers in the banking industry. Robo Advisors will save both wealth managers and customers a significant amount of time. Banks of the future will not only personalize their services and goods, but they will also use artificial intelligence to personalize their customers' experiences. When you walk into a bank branch, you will not be asked to show your identification card, but you will still be greeted by name, and the teller will be fully aware of the history of your bank accounts. This is a great example of the type of personalization that is possible with AI.

## HOW AI CAN BE USED TO BOOST ECONOMIC GROWTH FURTHER

According to the vast majority of studies, AI will have a significant impact on various aspects of the economy. Recent Accenture research predicts that AI will be able to quadruple yearly growth rates in the global economy by 2035, covering a total of 12 industrialized economies that collectively contribute more than 50 percent of the world's economic output (Accenture, 2016).

There are three major ways in which AI will propel this progress. To begin, it will result in a significant increase in labor productivity (by up to 40%), owing to the development of innovative technologies that will make workforce-related time management more efficient. Second, artificial intelligence will result in the creation of a new virtual workforce, dubbed "intelligent automation" by the researchers, capable of problem-solving and self-learning. Third, the economy will benefit from the spread of innovation, which will impact various industries and create new revenue streams. This will boost the global economy.

A study produced by PwC (PricewaterhouseCoopers), an international professional business services brand of firms, estimated that the rapid advancement and adoption of AI could lead to a 14 percent increase in global GDP (the equivalent of $15.7 trillion) by 2030. According to the study, the next wave of the digital revolution will be ushered in with the help of data generated by the Internet of Things (IoT), which is expected to be far greater than data generated by the current iteration of the "Internet of People (IoP)." The ability of people to connect and communicate with one another via the internet and other cognizant technologies is referred to as IoP. IoT will benefit from standardization and, as a result, automation, including the automation of personalization of goods and services. According to the PwC's analysis, there will be two primary channels through which AI will influence the global economy. The first possibility is that AI will lead to increased productivity in the work place. These advantages will be based on the automation of regular operations and are expected to have an impact on capital-intensive industries such as manufacturing and transportation. This will entail a greater use of various technological systems, such as robotics and self-driving cars. Firms that use AI technologies to supplement and support their existing staff will also see an increase in productivity. It will necessitate investing in software, systems, and machines based on assisted, autonomous, and augmented intelligence; which will not only enable the workforce to perform its tasks better and more efficiently, but will also free up time, allowing employees to focus on more stimulating and value-added activities. Because of automation, the demand for human labor would be reduced, resulting in higher levels of productivity.

The second channel involves the availability of artificial intelligence-enhanced products and services. Because the availability of personalized and higher-quality AI-enhanced products and services is likely to increase consumer demand, which will generate more data, the second channel will become even more important in the future. As PwC puts it, "increased consumption produces a vicious cycle of more data touchpoints and, as a result, more data, better insights, and better goods, and, as a result, more consumption." (PWC, 2018). Although the benefits will be felt globally, it is expected that China and North America will benefit the most from AI technology.

North America will almost certainly launch several productive technologies in the near future, and the gains will be boosted by advanced artificial intelligence usage (on the part of both enterprises and consumers), rapid data accumulation, and improved data driven understanding of customers.

Although China appears to be the leader in automation, as evidenced by increased data generation and AI implementation, it is likely that the country's massive manufacturing sector will be the first to realize the full impact of artificial intelligence, and it will then move up the value chain into more sophisticated and high-tech-driven manufacturing and commerce, if not already. Europe will also benefit greatly from AI, whereas poorer countries will likely see more modest gains due to lower rates of AI adoption.

The US will also experience significant economic gains from AI. According to the projections of McKinsey Global Institute (MGI), the business and economics research arm of McKinsey, more than 70% of organizations in the US will implement at least one form of artificial intelligence technology by 2030 (McKinsey Global Institute, 2018).

MGI further projects that artificial intelligence could result in an increase of approximately $13 trillion US dollars in economic output worldwide by 2030, resulting in an annual increase of approximately 1.2 percent in global GDP. This will primarily be due to automation replacing labor and an increase in the rate of innovative product and service development. On the other hand, some sources propose that artificial intelligence will have a limited impact on growth, as evidenced by sectors with the highest productivity growth rates but a declining overall share of the economy.

Also, AI could cause a shock in the labor markets, as well as the associated costs required to manage labor market transitions. This shock would be caused by negative externalities such as a decrease in domestic consumption as a result of unemployment.

Despite AI's advancement, some areas of the economy will remain critical and difficult to improve using AI, requiring well-paid human labor. In the end, this would prevent new technology from having a widespread impact on these sectors of the economy. It is also possible that AI will stifle future innovations because it will accelerate imitation, reducing the return on invention.

As a result, AI is likely to have both positive and negative effects on the economy. It remains to be seen whether the positive will outweigh the negative.

# Chapter Summary

We've seen how AI has changed the game in terms of data analysis and making the best decisions for increasing productivity and efficiency. Artificial intelligence is already affecting practically every business function across all industries. As a result, economic growth for many businesses could be astronomical, contributing to a new source of revenue for the global GDP.

The economy will benefit from the diffusion of innovation, which will have an effect on various industries and create new revenue streams, as well as from significant improvements in labor productivity and the creation of a new virtual workforce.

AI is the logical solution for businesses given the vast amount of data available today and the projected growth in data generation in the future. However, our reliance on it may change our world in ways we never imagined or anticipated.

Global competition for its advantages is fierce, and with the United States and Asia emerging as global leaders, many countries may fall further behind, creating an even greater economic gap than we have now.

In the future, artificial intelligence will pervade every industry and job sector. It has the potential to create new jobs in machine learning, data mining and analysis, AI software development, program management, and testing. With the advancement of AI, the demand for

AI-certified professionals is expected to rise. Because artificial intelligence is expected to play an increasingly important role in the information technology industry, obtaining certification in the field may provide you with a competitive advantage over other IT professionals. In general, it is difficult to predict where artificial intelligence will go in the future. There is no denying, however, that the opportunities provided by artificial intelligence (AI) can open up for those who invest in it.

## Digital Gold Nuggets

♦ *Artificial intelligence is a term that everyone is familiar with, and in some cases is even present in their homes (hello Alexa, Siri, Google Home, Cortana!).*

♦ *You can change the privacy settings on these devices and mobile phones to prevent them from listening in on your every conversation or recoding your voice.*

♦ *Let's not be afraid of the future. It is already here; AI-powered services and types of equipment and devices, such as drones, autonomous vehicles, and robots are all around us, to make our lives more convenient and productive.*

♦ *Explore and discover how you will be able to benefit from AI-powered services mentioned in this chapter.*

♦ *Invest in artificial intelligence (AI) education and training for your future.*

# Chapter Six

# SOCIAL MEDIA AND YOU

Social media is defined by its interactivity, connectivity, and user-generated content. In today's culture, social media usage has become a daily requirement. Two of the most common uses of social media are decision-making and social engagement. Social media is one of the best ways to connect with people both locally and globally. Social media can influence consumer purchasing decisions in a variety of ways, including reviews, marketing strategies, and paid advertising. Essentially, social media has a significant impact on our ability to interact, form connections, acquire and disseminate information, and make decisions.

Here, we will discuss the impact of social media (both good and bad) and how it is used, as well as habits and patterns observed from its various applications. However, we will go into greater detail about social media later on in the book, particularly as it relates to your data.

According to various reports including a report by Statista Research & Analysis, a leading provider of market and consumer data, more than half of the world's population has a social media account, with Facebook having nearly three billion users (Statista, 2022). Furthermore, there are five billion Internet users, or roughly three-quarters of the world's population, who use the Internet.

## HOW SOCIAL MEDIA IS INFLUENCING OUR LIVES

Regularly using social media has a number of advantages, many of which you are probably already aware of. If you use social media on a regular basis, you've probably encountered some or all of the following at some point in your life.

### 1.  Creating and Maintaining Personal Relationships

Connecting with others who share your interests on social media is a great way to meet new people. A sense of belonging in a small group of like-minded people can benefit us all. Social media platforms such as Facebook and Twitter have made it much easier to stay in touch with loved ones who have moved away. It's simple to stay in touch when you have a variety of communication options at your disposal.

You can connect with new people and start building relationships with them on social media. There are no boundaries to how far you can communicate and exchange information with your online friends. Because of its ability to bring people together, digital media has a distinct advantage in terms of connectivity.

## 2. Finding Your Voice

Anyone, regardless of age, can use social media to reach a larger audience than they would have otherwise. As a result, people can gain confidence, learn new communication methods, and quickly disseminate valuable information. Through TikTok, teenagers and young adults have created massive platforms from which they frequently communicate with tens of thousands, if not millions, of people. The cost and barrier to entry are extremely low.

## 3. Compassion and Generosity in Action

People aren't afraid to share their deepest thoughts and feelings on social media platforms such as Facebook, Instagram and Twitter. When you can relate to others, messages and comments can be used to demonstrate empathy. It can demonstrate to people you care about (and others you've never met) that you're interested in and sympathetic to their point of view. Seeing people persevere in the face of adversity may inspire and enlighten us.

## 4. Providing Assistance to Others

Social media can be used to support or promote a cause in which you strongly believe. Whether you're starting a new business, displaying your photography, or writing poems, those who share your interests may be able to assist you. It provides an opportunity to get to know others in your field and share your knowledge.

### 5. Improved Interactions

On social media, new topics are frequently discussed. Conversations that appear to be divisive and contentious may actually be an excellent opportunity to discuss important issues with people you care about and trust. If you're passionate about something, you can join a group dedicated to it.

### 6. Information Dissemination

On social media, news can spread quickly from anywhere in the world. Although this can be overwhelming at times, it can also keep us informed of important events. If you need to quickly spread the word about something, this can be a huge help. A person from a small town, for example, could use social media to spread the word about a lost dog. Everyone in the neighborhood would be able to keep an eye out for suspicious activity and report it immediately.

### 7. For Businesses

As a new business, you can use social media to spread the word about your exceptional products and services. By sharing relevant content, you can develop a brand voice that is appealing to your target audience. Businesses of all sizes can use social media to develop their markets and succeed with the help of online marketing and promotion.

### 8. Developing a Trusting Environment

You can start building trust and authority on social media by sharing expert information and connecting with individuals and other brands. As a result of your efforts, more and more people will learn about your fantastic company and its service.

## 9.  Increasing the Number of Visitors to Your Website

If one of your social media marketing goals is to increase inbound traffic, you can share useful information and advertising that directs visitors to your website. By distributing more valuable content on your website, you can increase traffic, leads, and sales. Advertising can be used to run campaigns that specifically target your current audience or people with similar goals.

## 10.  Providing a Superior Customer Experience

Businesses can benefit from using social media to improve the customer experience as well. To make your fans feel appreciated, respond to comments and inquiries as soon as possible. Using your social media accounts to demonstrate excellent customer service will help you gain attention and trust. Customers know they can come to you for help if they require anything you have to offer (with their credit cards ready!).

## 11.  Inspiring the Next Generation

On the Internet, you can find many successful businesses, entrepreneurs, and social media influencers. This will be especially encouraging for students and young professionals with big ideas and goals. Many influencers will publicly share their knowledge in order to help others thrive. You can improve your life by surrounding yourself with people who encourage you to live your values, dream big, and make a difference in the world.

## 12. Creativity

If you're an artist or work in the creative industry, social networking is a great place to share your work. You can count on people to be honest with you. Negative feedback is unavoidable, but social media experts must learn to tune out the haters.

Again, you may meet others who share your interests and can offer support and guidance in a specific area. You can make new friends and learn from their experiences. If you're brave enough to share your passion with the world, you might be able to make a living from it!

## 13. Social Media's Negative Effects

You may be surprised to learn that the negative effects of social media are both physical and mental. They have the power to shape your perception of the world and of yourself. While social media has some advantages, and there are many wonderful social media stories, it also has a significant number of disadvantages.

Are you still not convinced? Listed below are some of the negative effects of social media. If any of the following are issues in your personal life, consider limiting your use of social media:

## 14. Both Depression and Anxiety

Do you spend a lot of time per day scrolling through your various social media accounts? If you spend too much time on social networking sites, your disposition may suffer. In fact, regular social media users are more likely to report poor mental health, which may include symptoms of despair and anxiety.

The reason for this requires little mental effort to deduce. You can only see the highlights of other people's lives that have been meticulously curated on social media, which you can then contrast with your own shortcomings. The practice of judging oneself in relation to others is one of the surest ways to induce feelings of anxiety and dissatisfaction, and the rise of social media has only facilitated this tendency.

The question is, how can you use social media without causing yourself emotional distress? According to the same study (as well as good old-fashioned common sense), the amount of time you should spend on social media each day should be around half an hour. The key, as with many other potential problems that may arise in life, is moderation.

If you notice yourself becoming depressed after using social media, consider the networks you use as well as the people you follow. Politics and doomsday predictions are far more likely to make you nervous than music videos from your favorite artists.

## 15. Cyberbullying

Bullying could only occur in a direct confrontation with the victim prior to the advent of social media. Individuals, on the other hand, can now harass others online, whether anonymously or not. In today's world, everyone is aware of what cyberbullying is, and most of us have seen the harm it can cause to an individual.

Even though social media makes it easier to meet new people and make new friends, it also allows some users to be harsh and criticize others with little effort. For example, bullies can conceal their identities behind the anonymity provided by social media, gain their victim's trust, and then humiliate their victims in front of their peers. For example, they may create a phony profile and appear friendly toward another student, only to later betray and shame that student online.

These online attacks on people frequently leave severe psychological scars and, in some cases, even cause people to harm themselves or take their own lives. Adults, it turns out, are vulnerable to online bullying as well. When adults use the Internet, they can also face abuse and harassment. Because screens obscure our faces, it is possible to become jerks on social networking platforms and other websites without even realizing it.

## 16.  The Fear of Missing Out

The term "fear of missing out" (FOMO) refers to a phenomenon that became popular around the same time that social media usage became more widespread. Unsurprisingly, this is one of the most pervasive and widespread negative effects of social media on society. The fear of missing out (or FOMO) is exactly what it sounds like: anxiety caused by the fear of missing out on a great experience that someone else is having at the same time. For example, you may have a habit of frequently checking your messages to see if anyone has invited you out, or you may spend the entire day checking your Instagram feed to ensure that no one is having fun without you. It's also possible that you'll see images of something fun that your friends were able to do and feel left out because you couldn't join them due to another commitment.

This anxiety is constantly fueled by the content you come across on social media. The more you use social media, the more likely it is that you will come across someone who is now having a better time than you are. This is the source of the worry about missing out (FOMO).

## 17. Expectations that Cannot be Fulfilled

The majority of people are probably aware that using social media can lead to the formation of unrealistic expectations about life and friendships in one's head.

The vast majority of social media platforms are severely lacking in online authenticity. People will write on Facebook about how much they adore their significant other, and if they use Instagram, they will fill their Instagram profile with heavily staged photographs.

In reality, there is no way for you to tell whether or not this is all a charade. Even if everything appears to be in order on the surface, the person in question could be drowning in debt, their relationship with their significant other could be on the rocks, and they could be seeking validation through their Instagram likes.

## 18. A Poor Self-image of One's Body

When it comes to Instagram celebrities, it's worth noting that if you look through some of the most popular Instagram accounts, you'll see very beautiful people posing in expensive clothing on their well-proportioned bodies.

And it's no surprise that almost everyone is concerned about their appearance these days. Seeing images of so many people who are supposed to be ideal (according to societal norms) on a daily basis can undoubtedly make you aware of how your appearance differs from those images.

It's important to remember that everyone is a human being. No one wakes up every morning looking like a supermodel, and while many people have worked hard to train their bodies, that isn't always the case for everyone who appears to be in good shape. Many people have clearly gone down unhealthy paths in order to appear more appealing in the pursuit of social media popularity. Others have done expensive cosmetic procedures to enhance their appearance.

You won't have to worry about whether or not you appear to be beautiful on Instagram if you surround yourself with people who appreciate you for who you are.

## 19.  Unhealthy Sleep Habits

Aside from increasing the risk of developing anxiety and depression, spending too much time on social media platforms can make it difficult to get enough sleep, which is another disadvantage of these platforms. A greater amount of time spent on social media platforms has been shown in several studies to have a negative impact on sleep quality.

If you believe your sleep patterns have become erratic, resulting in a decrease in productivity, try to reduce the amount of time you spend on social media in order to get more sleep.

This is especially true if you use your phone in bed while it is dark outside. Many people make the mistake of telling themselves they'll only check their Facebook alerts for five minutes, only to discover an hour later that they'd been aimlessly scrolling through some nonsense on Twitter.

Do not allow the algorithms on social media platforms that are designed to keep your attention for as long as possible while also stealing your essential sleep to do so. Combining factors that contribute to poor sleep quality, with a reduction in overall sleep time can be dangerous to your health.

It's possible that social media is more addictive than smoking or drinking. It has a strong pull on many people, causing them to check it constantly without even thinking about it because it is so compelling.

Stop using social media if you discover that it is affecting your health and other aspects of your life negatively. If, on the other hand, you decide to stay, make a conscious decision to spend less time mindlessly scrolling through social media and, as a result, maintain a healthy relationship with it.

# Chapter Summary

Social media has a significant impact on our ability to interact, form connections, acquire and disseminate information, and make decisions. Anyone, regardless of age or demographics, can use social media to reach a larger audience than they would have otherwise. Social media can be used to promote a cause or to provide assistance to others. Businesses can use social media to promote their products and services. You can start following people who inspire and support you on social media if you're an entrepreneur.

Businesses can benefit from enhancing the consumer experience through the use of social media. Negative comments are unavoidable, but social media professionals must learn to ignore them. Social media has both physical and mental health consequences, as it is easier for people to compare themselves to others. This can result in anxiety, dissatisfaction, and cyberbullying.

The key is moderation; you should spend no more than half an hour per day on social media. You can become a jerk on social media without even realizing it. Fear of missing out (FOMO) is the source of the anxiety you experience when you are afraid of missing out on someone else's good time. Instagram celebrities pose in designer outfits on their well-proportioned bodies. Seeing images of so many people who are supposed to be ideal (according to societal norms) can make you aware of how your appearance differs from those images.

As a result of this circumstance, not everyone derives positive effects from using social media. Excessive time spent on social media platforms has been shown in a number of studies to have a negative impact on sleep quality. This is especially true if you use your phone in bed while it is dark outside. Because social media may be more addictive than smoking or drinking, you should monitor and control how much time you spend on it.

## Digital Gold Nuggets

♦ *Social Media can be addictive as any drug.*

♦ *Learn more about the effects of social media on your health and well-being, and limit your time spent on various platforms.*

♦ *Use a mobile app to track screen time and social media usage, and then set daily time limits (i.e. One hour per day).*

# Chapter Seven

# A NEW SOCIAL SCORING

That social media photo of you looking a little rough after a night out may make you laugh, but it could make it much more difficult for you to get a job in the financial and governmental services as governments and businesses are increasingly assessing you based on your social media behavior.

Businesses and governments are also increasingly using social scoring systems to assess the trustworthiness of consumers and others who have access to their services. Credit rating scores, which assist to evaluate a person's ability to repay debt and are already having an influence on people's ability to access financial services, are comparable to this notion. Furthermore, as a society, we are beginning to judge one another based on our online profiles, the digital image we project and the digital footprint we leave behind.

Imagine for a moment that every action you take, every interaction you have, and every movement you make could be summarized by a single rating on a scale of five points. If you have a low rating, it is possible that you will be isolated from the rest of society. On the other hand, if you have a high rating, you will have access to wonderful opportunities and unique advantages. This is what a social rating or social scoring system is all about.

In fact, similar systems exist in China, where its society is heavily monitored and tracked digitally through face recognition, digital wallets, and regular surveillance.

The social credit system that the Chinese government has proposed is one of the most well-known. However China, is not the only country that is implementing social monitoring solutions. According to new research, it was just recently revealed by the government of the United Kingdom that they would be using live facial recognition software on the streets of London in order to find suspects that are wanted by the police (nytimes.com, 2020). Similar systems are already utilized by law enforcement agencies and government organizations in other parts of the world, including China, Japan, Russia, UAE, US, and Brazil, to name a few. Numerous non-governmental entities, including many insurance companies located all over the world, have either announced or deployed systems that will enable its operators to effectively gather information about the behavior of individuals for the purpose of using it in significant decision-making processes. For instance, in the state of New York, life insurers are permitted to make decisions regarding their customers based on the information found in social networks. Information obtained from a tracking device that has been purposefully installed in a vehicle can be used by the auto insurance industry to devise new methods for determining the fees that should be charged for coverage.

There are technical solutions that enable proprietors of businesses such as restaurants to compile "blacklists" of individuals who are not permitted to enter their establishments due to previous instances of inappropriate behavior. Services that are part of the sharing economy, such as Airbnb, Uber and similar taxi services, and delivery services, all use some kind of scoring system to evaluate the people who participate in the service from a variety of perspectives.

## WHAT WE KNOW AT THIS POINT

The basic idea behind implementing a social rating system on a national scale is not particularly complicated: each individual citizen begins with a given score, and certain behaviors can either bring your score down or raise it higher. As an illustration, making a contribution to charity would raise your score, whereas purchasing cigarettes would bring it down. The rating of an individual can then determine whether or not they receive a reward or a punitive result. Potentially if a person's score falls below a certain threshold, for instance, the government may place restrictions on their ability to travel, prevent them from enrolling in the most prestigious universities, or even remove a pet from their care.

The majority of the rating systems that are in use today are constructed using massive amounts of historical data and machine learning models that make predictions about the future actions and outcomes of system participants. For instance, Microsoft employs such models to rank the skill level of players in online games; banks assess the validity of potential borrowers when they submit applications for loans; and a number of businesses have attempted to automate the process of reviewing resumes for open positions in their organizations.

Two of the most pressing unanswered questions are what the system would look like if fully implemented and how it would operate technologically. There are several possible explanations for this uncertainty.

To begin with, the system's designers are aware that the more information they share about it, the more holes others can poke in its security.

Second, it is entirely possible that the developers of the system do not themselves have a complete understanding of how it operates. They may simply be placing their faith in the reliability of their algorithms.

## HERE'S MY OUTLOOK ON WHAT A RANKED SOCIETY WILL LOOK LIKE

The description that follows are what I image might happen in practice. Every aspect of a person's life, from their eligibility to ride public transportation to the types of jobs they might be offered in the future, could be determined by a single score under the premise of a nationwide social score system. When this is done, the score ends up being the main factor that determines a person's place in society. If this occurs, the most likely result will be an increase in the degree of social stratification. The three factors that make up the foundation of social stratification are wealth, power, and prestige. In fact, the social ranking system will have a direct impact on these three factors.

**Wealth**: It's likely that a child born to parents with low financial standing won't get the chance to enroll in a reputable, high-priced school or university. As a consequence of this, the child has a much lower chance of obtaining a decent education and getting a good job with a good salary, which will severely limit their potential income in the future. On the other hand, an individual who has a good social score because of charitable donations (for example), will have access to the best jobs, which means that they can always maintain a steady rating by continuing to donate to charitable organizations.

**Power**: When it comes to power, a citizen who has a low social rating has a decreased chance of being able to hold a management position in either state or commercial enterprises. As a result, power remains concentrated in the hands of those who devised the ranking system in the first place and established the guidelines for determining how points are earned. This decreases the chances of breaking through the glass ceiling.

**Prestige**: One of the primary tools that the administrators of the various social scoring systems that are in use today use to exercise control is the concept of prestige. The opposite of this is the public shaming that can be inflicted on individuals. Information about "undesirable citizens" located in a particular area will be made available to the public, and even people who are not regarded as "undesirable" but communicate with those individuals will most likely have their own rating reduced as a result. People who have low social ratings will be excluded from society, and as a direct consequence of this, they will have no chance to improve their standing. Those who were either born into the top rankings or got to the top through purchasing their way there will always hold the most prestige.

In summary, in a world where our lives are based on a virtual score card, it is likely that as time goes on, the gap between people who have high ratings and those who have low ratings will continue to widen, resulting in a society that is extremely stratified. Those who begin at the bottom are much more likely to remain there throughout the entire process.

For even deeper understanding of the topic, let's take a look at these scenarios.

## MOVIES THAT MAKE YOU THINK

There are a number of films on the impact of technology on our future lives, particularly as it relates to data and AI, however, two films come to mind as examples of how this social rating system could work in the future; "Nosedive" is a Netflix Twilight Zone episode and "In Time," starring Justin Timberlake and Amanda Seyfried.

Nosedive is a 2015 Black Mirror episode from the Netflix Twilight Zone series. It's about a young lady named Lacie who lives her life in order to gain points on social media.

Although it is a fictitious world in which people are completely reliant on their score, the plot makes sense when you realize that almost all of the examples given are taken directly from our daily lives today.

"It's a satire on acceptance and the image of ourselves that we like to portray and project to others," says Charlie Broker, the episode's creator and writer.

Everything Lacie does is to raise her social standing. She is obsessed with her rating, which she constantly monitors and manipulates by rating people she knows with 5 stars in the hope that they will return the favor.

Every time she does something that affects her score, the show projects her score on the screen, and her emotions are ruled and influenced by her score.

Of course, everyone in her world can read each other's scores because they all wear special contact lenses that allow them to look at someone and see their rating, similar to a holographic projection. Every upload and interaction is rated by the platform's users, yielding an average score out of 5. This is the 5-point or 5-stars system used by hotels, Uber for their drivers and the online gaming community to rate gamers.

Anything higher than a 4 is considered excellent. Ratings between 3 and 4 are still acceptable, but anything less than 3 is considered unacceptable because it lowers one's social standing and affects one's ability to obtain quality service or access to privileges that those with higher ratings have.

You see, a person's worth in Lacie's world is determined by their rating, so as a result, she works tirelessly to improve her score. Despite the fact that she suffers from severe insecurities and is generally unhappy with her life, she decides to seek the assistance of a social media consultant so that she can improve her score. He uses in-depth analytics and algorithms to compare her profile to those on the platform, and he comes to the conclusion that in order for her to live the life of her dreams, she need only engage in conversations with a select group of high-value individuals.

However, it all falls apart because she creates a world in which she is so inauthentic that, instead of receiving a higher rating, she ends up receiving a lower rating on each subsequent encounter she has, mostly due to circumstances and situations beyond her control, as people see right through her inauthenticity with every interaction.

It's an uncanny and parallel representation of the social media-driven world we live in today. It's how we try to get other people to respond and like what we want, by projecting our own desires onto them.

This highlights the dangers of measuring our self-worth based on the opinions and assessments of others. Now-a-days, it seems like much of our lives are influenced by those we follow and value on social media platforms; frequently, these are celebrity figures whose social score is projected as higher in our minds due to the lifestyle they project on these platforms. Those with high ratings tend to receive high ratings from others and, as a result, form and remain members of social groups with similar ratings.

Is this something you've heard before? It's the human condition, and it can be seen in society with or without social media, and it's influenced by a person's socioeconomic status. The more privileges and opportunities they have access to, the better.

The main difference is that technology now allows us to easily score each other based on our online behavioral habits and patterns.

Another film that depicts the impact of technology on our future lives is "In Time." Andrew Niccol wrote and directed the 2011 science fiction film In Time, starring Justin Timberlake and Amanda Seyfried. It depicts a social system based on an embedded biological digital clock.

This takes place in the future, when time is the only valuable commodity. People have a clock embedded in their wrist, and when it reaches zero, they die. The premise is that after the age of 25, the ageing gene shuts down and they only have a year to live. However, the body clock imprinted on the left forearm does not start ticking until they reach the age of majority (i.e. 25 years of age). As a result, they are safe until their 25th birthday. So, while everyone wants to know how to stay 25 forever, there is always the possibility that something will go wrong.When the clock begins to tick, the poor must work to gain more time. However, the wealthy can buy time. So, it clearly becomes a class struggle, with the wealthy having millions of hours to do whatever they want. Time is literally money in this world.

As a result of running out of time, everyone has the ability to create, steal, buy or borrow time; all of this is transmitted via your pulse in your left arm.

Of course, there are the class enforcement officers and the policing of where and how people obtain and use any extra time gained. All of this is made possible and supported by a world of digitally centralized data to monitor and control its population and societies.

Justin Timberlake's character plays an ordinary slum resident who wakes up every day with only 23 hours on the clock, implying that he has less than a day to live and is forced to run the hamster wheel in order to survive one more day. While Amanda plays a character from a wealthy part of town who has all the time in the world. The two form a tragic forbidden relationship of the classes that leads to the film's climax.

It's a fascinating concept as the data basically underpins society's activities, and makes it all possible. Although the movie is primarily concerned with the social class structure. These data elements make you believe that this is a real thing or situation that could happen. It obviously looks to the future, as most science fiction does, but it also speaks to the present and where we could go from here.

In this film, there are people who have a lot of time and people who have little time, resulting in a social ladder in which the two groups of people live in very different worlds. People with a lot of time can afford to buy more time to extend their lives, whereas people with a limited amount of time are stuck in society's wastelands, waiting to die as their time runs out.

Now, although these two films highlight the real possibilities of tomorrow's world we might find ourselves in that world sooner than we think given that all of the technology exists and is in place, although mass adoption is still required to make it a reality.

# Chapter Summary

We are beginning to judge one another as a society based on our online profiles, the digital image we project, and the digital footprint we leave behind. This is the purpose of a social rating or social scoring system. Similar systems are already in use by law enforcement and government agencies all over the world. The concept of a national social rating system is not particularly complicated or far-fetched.

Two of the most pressing unanswered questions are how the system will look in practice and how it will operate technologically. The system's designers are aware that the more information they share about it, the more holes it creates in its security. When a social credit system determines a person's place in society, the degree of social stratification is likely to increase. The gap between people with high ratings and those with low ratings will continue to grow over time. The Netflix Twilight Zone Nosedive episode and the In Time film show how this could work in the future.

## Digital Gold Nuggets

♦ *That photo of you looking a little rough after a night out on social media may make you laugh, but it could make it much harder for you to obtain financial and governmental services as governments and businesses increasingly assess you based on your social media behavior.*

*♦ Take some time to go through your online posts and delete anything that you are not proud of or that does not accurately represent you.*

*♦ Be cautious about what you post or say online! (Remember that your data leaves a permanent digital footprint).*

# Chapter Eight



We are all aware of the negative effects that data breaches can have on organizations, ranging from regulatory fines, reputational damage, and share price declines to the costs of investigating and compensating victims. You must have wondered at some point how these breaches affect individuals and why we should be concerned.

The most important reason for safeguarding our devices and Internet accounts is to protect our personal and financial identities. Phishing scams, which trick people into disclosing personal information, are becoming more common, and the more information we have publicly available on the Internet or social media, the more likely we are to fall victim to one of these scams.

As a defense for less sensitive information, some people find it easier to think, "I have nothing to hide, so it doesn't matter." But, in reality, everyone has something to hide, whether it's how much money we made last year or how many episodes of our favorite TV show we've seen.

You never know what the future has in store for us, no matter how confident you are right now. To put it another way, each of us should be able to decide how much of our information people can access online.

One of the most common responses to cybersecurity concerns is to simply ignore it. No one would want your personal information if you weren't a high-ranking government official or the owner of a multi-million-dollar bank account, right?

Unfortunately, this is not the case. According to a survey by Pew Research Center, nearly everyone owns a smartphone, and more than three-quarters of adults own multiple Internet-connected devices (Mobile Fact Sheet, 2022). Consider how much time you spend on your smartphone and other electronic devices to understand why this is significant. Smartphone users frequently engage in online shopping, bill payment, and even the use of a social security or social insurance number. As a result, it's vital that you exercise caution when it comes to safeguarding your private information.

Despite the fact that your smartphone is the most frequently used device, you most likely use a variety of other devices at home and at work. Your actions on these websites have an impact on everyone who uses the network, not just you. A network's password is the most common entry point for cybercriminals. As a result, if you have poor security practices in one area, a cybercriminal could gain access to additional data on your device or network. Personal information security is a technique for becoming more aware of the dangers posed by cyberattacks on all devices.

## WHO SHOULD IMPLEMENT BETTER PROCEDURES TO PROTECT THEIR PERSONAL INFORMATION?

Everyone should do everything possible to safeguard their data. If you aren't already taking every precaution to keep your personal information secure across all of your devices, you may be putting yourself at risk. Because of the convenience of technology, it's all too easy to overlook or minimize security precautions in order to quickly access the apps and websites you enjoy. Unfortunately, the activities you engage in that allow you to take shortcuts also allow hackers access to your personal information for malicious purposes.

## WHERE TO IMPLEMENT CYBERSECURITY BEST PRACTICES

One common misconception among Internet users is that cybersecurity is only a concern when using public computers. This is a complete fabrication. Cybercriminals who attack critical networks are frequently not in the same country as the organizations they are attempting to harm. A personal gadget is used to launch attacks from a safe distance. If criminals can break into government agencies and large corporations, your home or business network will be no match. To avoid becoming a victim, you must take every precaution to safeguard your data. You should follow sound cybersecurity procedures in each of these cases. Here are some examples.

**The Public Domain:** The proliferation of mobile devices has created convenience by allowing shoppers to find exactly what they want and how to acquire it quickly. In many cases, this entails browsing the Internet in a public place, such as a store, before making a purchase. Despite the convenience of free public Wi-Fi, there are few security safeguards in place to protect against hackers.

**Your Working Environments:** Your company most likely has policies in place that require Internet security measures. Too many employees take shortcuts, use weak passwords, and use company equipment for personal gain. Proper security protocol is critical in the workplace, regardless of how you use the Internet (or what you use it for). It's possible that you're the backdoor through which an intruder enters.

**Your Personal Networks:** Even if you have a password-protected network at home, you should not relax your security measures. Scammers target people who use computers or mobile phones to access the Internet. It is critical to practice good security habits in order to avoid becoming a victim.

**Whenever You Go Online (regardless of where you are):** Public Wi-Fi or high-security networks are both affected by your actions and can make your personal information unsafe if you are not careful. The best way to keep your personal information safe on any network or device is to practice good cybersecurity habits.

## PERSONAL DATA SECURITY ON ALL DEVICES

You should follow all of the guidelines and best practices outlined in this book when it comes to securing your online information. A common misconception is that data protection regulations exist solely for high-tech firms and large organizations tasked with managing hundreds of thousands of clients' personal data. The primary targets of most threat actors are not major corporations or government entities. Criminals look for people who don't bother to take the necessary precautions when it comes to securing sensitive information. If you're completely new to cybersecurity and the actions requested for protecting your personal information, it's time to start from the beginning. The following tips can assist you in safeguarding your personal information.

## REMEMBER THAT YOU ARE A TARGET FOR HACKERS

Regardless of how small your bank account or client list is, there is always someone interested in the information you have to offer. The attackers do not have to breach every system that they target. They simply have to go to the ones that are the most accessible. This strategy can be used to break into critical systems and steal a person's identity. Instead of making your network more accessible, you should focus on tightening security to deter intruders.

## FOLLOW ALL PASSWORD RULES AND REGULATIONS

Nothing is more inconvenient than having to remember multiple passwords for each of your favorite websites. You'll forget what you just typed a few minutes later. As a result, in the future, there will be a need to look for a forgotten password. You can also quickly connect your smartphone to the standby mode (i.e. select sleep or screen timeout) that you use for all websites and apps. Follow these tips to make the most of the level of security provided by your passwords:

- Use a variety of characters, digits, and letters in your passwords rather than a single easily recognizable term.
- Never use the same password for more than one website or service.
- You should not use your social media credentials, email credentials, or any other account to log in to other websites.
- Make use of a password manager (i.e. software application that is designed to store and manage online credentials).
- When possible, use two-factor authentication (also referred to as 2FA) which only allows access after successfully presenting two or more pieces of evidence to authenticate your identity.

## TYPICAL SCAMS TO WATCH OUT FOR

The person who sends you spam texts and emails is likely to be someone you've never met. Often, they are simply crooks attempting to gain access to your personal information or your entire network. Phishing scams can be carried out through a variety of channels, including the phone, email, text message, and social networking websites. Typically, phishing scams involve attackers sending fraudulent emails or text messages disguised as legitimate in order to obtain your personal or sensitive information or to carry out some malicious intent. If you receive an unknown notification from one of your email accounts or text, do not click on the provided links; instead, use your browser to check your account to verify the information.

## PUT AN END TO YOUR HABIT OF IGNORING UPDATES

Installing software updates may appear to be a waste of time, but it is not. Keeping your apps and device software up to date ensures that you are protected from the most recent security threats. Software updates are frequently used to address previously discovered security flaws. Turn on automatic updates to keep your operating system up to date. Chrome, Firefox, and other browsers should be used because they receive regular automatic updates and keep extensions up to date.

## AVOID EXCESSIVE SOCIAL MEDIA POSTING

Social media is often treated as if it were a private conversation between friends. Even if you're not uploading images of your driver's license or credit cards, you may be revealing more information than you realize. Identity thieves can use information obtained from social media to answer personal security questions, locate their victims, and even obtain their birth dates or the birth dates of their children.

## BE CAREFUL WHAT YOU CLICK

Trusted websites exist for a reason. Use them! Malicious software can be found on websites that offer high-priced items or services at a low or no cost. Never install software from an unknown or untrusted source. Do not open attachments or click on links unless the sender is known to you, or there is nothing suspicious or unusual about the content and purpose of the communication have been verified.

## INSTALL AND CONFIGURE VIRUS PROTECTION SOFTWARE

It is not necessary to do everything on your own. Several well-known corporations provide security measures to protect your personal information across all of your devices. Before installing anti-virus software, make sure to get it from a reputable source. Your anti-virus software should be updated on a regular basis to ensure that you have the most up-to-date protection.

## ENCRYPTION CAN HELP YOU PROTECT YOUR DATA

Online transactions are extremely convenient and enable you to obtain products that you would not be able to obtain in your own neighborhood. When you use these services, cybercriminals may be able to gain access to your personal and financial information. You can make it difficult or impossible for others to decipher the information you send over the Internet by using data encryption. The presence of a lock icon in your browser's status bar indicates secure data transmission. Make sure the lock icon is visible before sending any sensitive data.

## ESTABLISH CONSISTENT PRIVACY PREFERENCES

When was the last time you double-checked the privacy settings on your email and social media accounts? You're not the only one who hasn't checked the settings on their accounts since they were created. As a result, you may be unaware of how much of your personal information is available for the taking.

Online shopping apps, social media platforms, and email services all have frequently changing privacy policies that you should be aware of. If you take the time to read the terms of service to understand these changes, you are in the minority. Check your policy changes and update the privacy settings on your account to avoid sharing personal information with websites and apps linked to social media accounts.

## SECURING YOUR DEVICES TO PROTECT YOUR PERSONAL DATA

On all devices, you can protect your personal information with optional security measures. In addition to following good cybersecurity practices, using the security features built into your devices will help you avoid revealing your personal information. Every new device should include instructions on how to keep your personal information safe while using that device. With these suggestions, you can take advantage of your device's built-in security features.

Examine the privacy statement: That lengthy and detailed page will explain how your smartphone shares your personal information with installed apps and websites you visit. You can use the settings to improve your privacy.

Make sure your phone or tablet is secure: Automatic login options make it simple to access data on your preferred device. They also make it easier for others to access your data. Use a strong password and a two-step verification mechanism to unlock your smartphone whenever possible. When not in use, always lock your smartphone.

Make use of device security software: Many smartphones come with pre-installed security software. Make it a point to learn how the provided security package compares to competing options. Install additional security software as needed to ensure complete security.

Before you throw away any type of computer or smartphone, delete all of your personal information:

Check the owner's manual or the manufacturer's website to learn how to completely erase your data from the device's hard disc.

Your personal information is only as secure as you make it. If you've never taken the necessary precautions in the past, implementing security measures can appear intimidating. Instead of procrastinating, focus on each step to develop habits that will soon become your only method of operation.

# Chapter Summary

Cyber identity theft and data breaches are two of the most common and negative consequences of Internet use, as well as the greatest threat to the current state of the Internet. Furthermore, our lax security and password management practices contribute to this threat by allowing easy access to our personal information and, in some cases, the intellectual property of our business or employers, including one of their most valuable assets, their data.

Indeed, the fact that we can access the Internet from virtually anywhere and at any time complicates cybersecurity, as criminals can break into government agencies, corporations, your home or business network from virtually anywhere and at any time, so lax personal security management on various networks, regardless of location and access points, can create critical opportunity for cybercriminals.

To avoid becoming a victim or a contributor, you must take every precaution to safeguard your data, such as protecting your personal data on all your devices with virus protection software and using encryption software. Also, be sure to take note of your social media footprint as well, as you may be unknowingly giving away personal identity information to unsuspecting criminals looking for such innocence. In addition, if you receive a notification from one of your accounts, instead of clicking on the provided links, use your browser to check your account to verify the information.

When it comes to protecting your personal information, you must be extremely cautious and vigilant. We don't know what the future holds for us, so regardless of how certain we are right now, each of us should be able to decide how much of our information people can access online.

## Digital Gold Nuggets

♦ *It's vital that you exercise caution when it comes to safeguarding your private information.*

♦ *Enable two-factor authentication (2FA) at all times to ensure that only authorized users can access your account. For most apps, this is simple as receiving a numeric code via text or email when you log-in to help verify your identity.*

♦ *Do not ignore the updates provided by Software, Apps and device manufacturers. Always update all your devices and computers regularly to avoid vulnerabilities. Also turn on automatic updates.*

♦ *When conducting financial transactions online, look for the lock icon in the status bar of your browser, which indicates secure data transmission. Before sending any sensitive information, make sure the lock icon is visible.*

# Chapter Nine

## MONETIZING YOUR DATA

This chapter will explore why our personal data is valuable; You've probably seen stories in the media about how search engines and social media platforms sell your personal information for a lot of money.

But have you considered selling your personal data to Microsoft, Twitter, Google, Pinterest, or Facebook? Such corporations already track every mouse movement you make, collecting data that is used by advertising companies to show you targeted ads based on your interests. However, do you really have to give your data away for free? You might as well make a couple of dollars yourself by monetizing this data, but before we get there, let's define data monetization. Here's a quick rundown:

Have you ever been distracted by an advertisement for an item of interest while using Facebook?

Advertisements that are specifically tailored to you are referred to as "targeted" ads. Tracking companies (or data brokers) use "cookies" to keep track of their customers:

- The websites you visit
- What you look at
- What you buy on the Internet
- Even what you post on your social media profiles

The data brokers may resell this information to other companies or keep it for their own use in determining which advertisements you see in the future. All of these companies are making billions of dollars off of your personal information, but the vast majority of us will never see a penny of it.

Which brings us back to our original question: What if we can?

In this chapter, we'll show you how to make a little extra money by selling your data online rather than giving it away for free, or how to use it as a corporate entity while adhering to the privacy rules.

## THE VALUE OF YOUR PERSONAL INFORMATION

Personal information has a market value. Every year, billions of dollars are spent on advertising on platforms such as Facebook and Google. In fact, both platforms receive more than half of all online marketing dollars. Hackers who are skilled at stealing and reselling data make a lot of money. A credit score company's profits are directly related to this.

Unless you're an outlier, everyone has gigabytes of digital data stored on their devices or in the cloud.

But how much does your data actually cost? Consider the value of some personal information to the average citizen. Let's break it down further using US statistical data.

## YOUR PERSONAL INFORMATION'S ADVERTISING VALUE

Advertisers are willing to pay a premium price for the privilege of capturing your attention. Facebook, Google, and other digital ad brokers, for example, use your information to target your ads. They track your habits and build a consumer profile of you (your demographics, preferences, lifestyle, stage of life, and various other attributes).

Because Facebook knows so much about its users, it can profit from that information. The average American spends about 40 minutes per day on the site. Facebook uses statistical algorithms on a regular basis to match consumers with products that advertisers hope to promote to them.

In 2017, the average cost of an online Facebook ad was $1.72 per click, a premium price due to Facebook's ability to analyze and deconstruct massive amounts of data.

Google, the other digital domain powerhouse, cannot compete with Facebook in this area, but compensates by controlling 80% of the US search advertising market through Google AdWords.

According to Wordstream, Google AdWords clicks averaged $2.32 in 2017 (Shewan, 2022). There are some clicks that are significantly more expensive. The price is determined through an auction, so it varies according to demand. In some cases, AdWords for legal services can cost more than $50 per click. If you can get your hands on it, it's a very nice piece of work.

If we divide the total US digital advertising income of $83 billion by the total number of American Internet users, we can easily calculate how much money companies spend on advertising to Americans individually. When calculated, it comes to a total of $289.19 per year for each American on an average. This is an average, so your total will be higher if you conduct a large number of product searches or click on a large number of website advertisements, which is especially true if you frequently seek legal services.

## WHAT IS THE EXTENT OF YOUR PERSONAL DATA INVENTORY?

Your personal data is probably more comprehensive than you think. It contains information like your name, address, phone number, and email address, as well as official documents proving your identity like a birth certificate, driver's license, passport, and so on.

Gender, age group or band, economic status (such as income level, property ownership, etc.), personal interests, hobbies, and preferences can be added on top of this, yielding data that is useful to both advertising and retail businesses. Cryptocurrency wallets are a relatively new addition to the list of financial data that can be accessed through a user's online account.

Past addresses, phone numbers, school records, transcripts, work records, certifications, and criminal histories are all examples of personal history. Not to mention your own personal history of buying and selling.

There is health information, such as your recent medical history, doctor's reports, lab results, and medications you've been taking (if any) too.

Memberships in any type of organization or group, such as sports clubs, retail warehouses, air mileage program, political affiliations, and so on, can also be incorporated.

We also need to include all of the digital rights that you manage, such as login information for websites, software apps, or digital services like Netflix or Amazon Prime.

This list can also include ownership information, deeds, titles, and provenance. Then there are your physical electronic goods, which include e-mails and other text files, photos, films, music, and other audio recordings. Finally, you have your own digital footprints, which are basically a record of everything you've ever done online.

## HOW TO BEGIN THE PROCESS OF SELLING YOUR INFORMATION

One method for monetizing your data is to sell it directly to another company or to participate in a data exchange. You can sell your data as a commodity or the knowledge that you gained from it.

## DIRECT SALE OF YOUR DATA

The most straightforward option is to sell your data to another company directly via a private transaction set up by either you or the other party. To use this strategy, you must either already have a relationship with a company interested in purchasing your data or conduct some research to find a potential buyer.

## CONNECT WITH OTHER PRIVATE MARKET BUYERS AND SELLERS

You could also participate in a private data marketplace, where businesses trade information. Transparent transactions allow high-end buyers to easily purchase your data. With this option, you'll have regular access to buyers you wouldn't have had otherwise.

## DATA AGGREGATORS ARE INTERESTED IN PURCHASING YOUR DATA

You could also sell your data directly to companies that will use it on an aggregate bases, such as a data aggregator or similar company. While using a third-party broker to sell a large amount of data is convenient, you may not get as good a price or have as much control over the transaction. Make sure the organization you partner with is trustworthy, secure, and capable before deciding to go this route.

When it comes to selling your data, you have a number of options. You can either sell the data itself or share the knowledge you've gained from studying it to make a profit. One benefit of selling insights rather than data is that you retain complete control over your data.

## SELLING YOUR DATA TO REPUTABLE WEBSITES

If you don't mind sharing your information and want to make money without doing much work, some of the websites listed below may be able to help you participate in the data-for-cash bonanza that is currently going on without your knowledge. You can earn money without doing much work if you don't mind sharing your information.

## HONEYGAIN

Even though it is not a data selling platform, Honeygain is a good way to supplement your income. It is a program that can be downloaded to your computer or Android phone. Following that, the application will use your Internet connection to conduct a variety of marketing research inquiries on behalf of their customers. Companies can benefit from market research like this, which is conducted across multiple locations and devices. They make no attempt to examine your data or conduct. They pay you for participating in the survey.

## NATIONAL CONSUMER PANEL (NCP)

The National Consumer Panel compiles data on your purchases. You are given either the NCP smartphone app or a handheld scanner, which you use to read barcodes on the products you purchase. You will then be able to accumulate points that can be redeemed for prizes and sweepstakes entries.

You can redeem your points for NCP gift catalogue merchandise, and the quarterly sweepstakes offer prizes worth up to $20,000 to the lucky winner. You can earn even more points by participating in surveys or participating in exclusive research. However, your data is aggregated and only available to their customers as market level consumer data. Under the data for points agreement, your personal data is never made available. IRI and Nielsen, both market research firms, offer similar services.

## DATACOUP

DataCoup bills itself as the "world's first personal data marketplace" and "the only company that helps you sell your anonymous data for real, cold hard cash," according to its website. This software allows you to connect to a variety of social networking platforms. Facebook, Twitter, LinkedIn, Instagram, and Tumblr are some of these platforms. You can also link a debit or credit card to your account to keep track of your spending habits. If you do this, your connection to your bank will be read-only, and your credentials will never be saved in any way.

You will be paid whenever one of your data sources sells for the market price, which is determined separately for each data source. You will be able to cash out your earnings once you have a balance of at least $5 in your account. The collection of earnings is stopped at $25 until you redeem your money. You will then be able to continue participating. You can load money onto a debit card that accepts either Visa or MasterCard.

So, in essence, there are dozens of similar platforms on the Internet that will buy your personal information. All you have to do is know where to look.

# Chapter Summary

We've seen how valuable your personal information is and how much it's worth in terms of money. We also discovered that Big Tech (also known as tech giants) makes a lot of money off of the personal information you freely give away online, and advertisers are hungry and willing to pay for such valuable information that allows them to hyper-target their audience like never before.

However, there is still a lot more money to be made as the digital world explodes with advertisement opportunities and requires more digital fuel to feed the advertisement engines, which is your data.

As a result, you can profit from your own personal data by selling it to companies who want to use it for ad targeting and other marketing services.

Advertisers will pay a premium to get your attention, as we've already established. Your information is used to target ads by Facebook, Google, and other digital ad brokers. We discovered that the average spent per year on digital advertising to American is $289.19 per year per person; if you frequently search for products or legal services, this figure may be higher.

Your personal history and digital footprint include past addresses, phone numbers, school records, work records, certifications, and criminal histories. E-mails and other text files, photos, films, music, and other audio recordings are also physical electronic items.

As previously stated, you can make money without doing much work if you don't mind sharing your information. Some of the websites we've listed may be able to help you participate in the current data-for-cash goldmine that's going on behind your back. These platforms include Facebook, Twitter, LinkedIn, Instagram, and Tumblr.

In addition, points can be accumulated and redeemed for items from the NCP, IRI, or Nielsen gift catalogues, and quarterly sweepstakes offer cash and prizes for participating in their data for prize programs.

DataCoup bills itself as the "world's first personal data marketplace," where you can sell your personal data in a secure, aggregated, and anonymized market.

After some investigation, we discovered that there are numerous ways to take control of your data, and if you want to leverage it for your own gain, you can do so through various platforms and data broker services. However, I strongly advise you to do more research before entering this ground.

## Digital Gold Nuggets

♦ *Data is one of today's most valuable commodity.*

♦ *Look into selling your data or the insights you gain from it to reputable organizations that use safe and secure data exchange.*

♦ *On reputable websites, you can also participate in the data-for-cash goldmine.*

# Chapter Ten



We can safely conclude that we are living in a social media era. According to Statista's recent study, there are approximately 4.6 billion active social media users worldwide, with the average user spending 145 minutes per day on social media (Statista, 2022). Furthermore, numerous Internet studies show that every smartphone user has at least one social media profile. That is astonishing. It means that more than half of the world's population spends more than an hour per day on social media, with those who have smartphones accessing at least one account.

Social media isn't just for interacting with friends and family; it's also a great place for businesses to find new customers and stay in touch with existing ones. These platforms enable businesses and individuals to post their ideas, images, or videos, and add an incomprehensible amount of data that grows exponentially with each passing year.

In this chapter, we will delve deeper into the benefits of social media for both professionals and individuals, as well as how data is generated through our use of social media.

## A BRIEF OVERVIEW OF SOCIAL MEDIA DATA

It should come as no surprise that the concept of privacy will almost certainly be considered archaic in the future. You can learn a lot about someone by browsing their social media accounts, thanks to the geolocation check-ins, tagged photos, event RSVPs, online timestamps, and other information they share. A person's social media data profile potentially contains all of the information that can be known about them, such as their political beliefs, relationship status, college alma mater, and any other readily shareable information.

People are almost always willing to hand over personal data to social media platforms such as Facebook and Twitter in exchange for access to those platforms. This allows for the mining and organization of all of this data in order to gain a better understanding of not only individual users but also entire user segments.

The term "social media data" refers to a wide range of online information, including photos, purchase history, active hours spent on social media, engagement rate with specific types of content, and a variety of other things. The story of the high school student who began receiving online coupons from the retailer Target for baby products is likely familiar to at least some of this book's readers. Before her father found out his daughter was expecting, he was enraged that Target had sent her coupons for baby products. However, he was unaware that she was pregnant at the time. Target discovered this information before he did by analyzing his daughter's search data and social media content.

## HOW CAN SOCIAL MEDIA DATA HELP BUSINESSES?

According to new research from ProPublica, Facebook "collected more than 52,000 unique attributes that Facebook has used to classify users" in 2016 (ProPublica, 2016). That is a lot of information about a single person. Most people couldn't even name 1,000 different characteristics about themselves, let alone 52,000 distinct characteristics. When marketers are presented with 52,000 distinct characteristics about just one person, they are frequently overwhelmed by the volume of data and are unsure what to make of it all (unless they are assisted by AI).

First, we will look at the different types of social media data points that are collected. Then we will consider how marketers can use this information for targeted communication with users and to build stronger relationships with them.

## WHAT KINDS OF SOCIAL MEDIA DATA DO SOCIAL PLATFORMS COLLECT?

The various types of data collected about social media platform users can be roughly classified into five distinct categories. These are the following categories: behavioral data, engagement data, personal data, attitude data, and preference data.

## DATA FROM BEHAVIORAL SOCIAL MEDIA

The advertiser must decide whether the desired action is for the user to make a purchase, or visit the advertiser's website, or share information on product via a website, or a social media post. Behavioral social media data looks for patterns that users frequently engage in while on their way to completing an action that advertisers desire.

The following are some examples of social media behavioral data points:

- Social Media Transactional Data: This includes subscriptions, purchases, previous purchases, cart abandonment data, average customer lifetime value, details about customer loyalty programs, and so on.
- The Social Media Usage: actions that are repeated, task completion, feature utilization, feature duration, various types of devices, and so on.

- Qualitative data gathered from social media platforms, such as user attention, heatmaps (clicks, scroll, and mouse movement data), time on site/time on app, and so on.

## DATA ON SOCIAL MEDIA ENGAGEMENT

Social Media networks collect and measure engagement data to track how users interact with their social media platform, third-party sites, and the platforms used by their advertisers.

The following are some examples of the types of engagement data metrics collected about social media users:

- Interactions between websites and mobile apps, such as website visits, app stickiness, most viewed pages, user flow, traffic sources, and so on.
- Post likes, post shares, post replies, native video views, and so on are all examples of social media platform engagement.
- Email engagement metrics include open rate, click-through rate, bounce rate, email forwards, and so on.
- Paid ad engagement metrics such as impressions, click-through rate, cost per click, ad conversions, and others.

## PERSONAL SOCIAL MEDIA DATA

The term "personal social media data" refers to information about a person's identity that, if compromised, could disclose that person's identity. Many of these data points are restricted from marketers in order to protect the user's identity and safety. Marketers, on the other hand, have access to data points that are less likely to reveal sensitive information, such as a user's birthday, gender, and age.

Here are a few examples of personal data found on social media:

- Name, either first or last name, or full name
- Location: a country, state, city, or specific location, along with a ZIP or postal code or an exact physical address
- Email address
- Phone number
- Usernames and/or passwords required for logging in
- Driver's license number
- Social security number
- Passport number
- Date and time of birth
- Credit card or debit card details
- Age, gender, race, and ethnicity
- Specific ages or age groups
- Information about their current position as well as work history

# SOCIAL MEDIA ATTITUDE DATA

At its most basic, attitudinal social media data refers to information about the sentiments and feelings of social media users. This information assesses how users perceive specific messages, different types of social media content, and other types of information. Due to the subjective nature of the data, attitudinal data is typically collected through the use of polls, surveys, interviews, user feedback, user complaints, reviews, and other similar methods.

The following are some examples of attitude data that can be collected about social media users:

- The driving forces that motivate the user and the obstacles that they face
- User gratification
- User sentiments
- Aspects of the social network that users consider desirable
- User preferences
- Purchase requirements or preferences

## DATA ON SOCIAL MEDIA PREFERENCES

On social media platforms, "preference data" refers to how a user identifies or supports various activities, ideas, content, included on the platform and so on. Some examples of social media preference data that a user may have are as follows:

- Political affiliation
- Religious beliefs

- Personal food preferences
- Favorite activities
- Movies and television shows
- Favorite sports teams

## WHAT ARE SOME EFFECTIVE WAYS TO USE SOCIAL MEDIA DATA?

The majority of the time, social media user data is used to deliver hyper-targeted advertisements to users while they are on social media networks.

Companies determine which data points from social media are most important by answering the following questions:

- Who exactly constitutes my ideal clientele?
- Which social networks do they use on a regular basis?
- How do they interact with the various social media networks?

By following the answers to these questions, it is much easier to zero in on the social media data that will be most useful in better understanding the target audience.

As an example:

A company sells specialty cakes, and one of their target customers is the parents of children under the age of 16. Following a review of engagement and behavioral data from adults aged 25 to 45, they conclude that the adults who comprise the target audience spend the majority of their time on Facebook and Instagram, with only a small amount of time spent interacting on Twitter. They use the platforms to stay in touch with friends, read the news, laugh at funny videos and pictures, and share photos of their children and families.

That's a good start toward learning more about a customer's ideal demographic, which is a critical step. Now that the advertisers know which social media data points will be useful, they can better target and engage the audience that they want to gain access to this information.

The following are some examples of preference data points that will help the company learn more about its target customers and reach them:

- Favorite sports teams
- Favorite films or television shows
- Vacation destinations
- Food preferences (including diets and food allergies)

Using this data, a cake company could create targeted advertisements for user groups who are fans of the Star Wars films and shows, by offering custom Star Wars-themed cakes. These advertisements could target users who are interested in purchasing Star Wars-themed cakes. And with that, the company has the potential to become a more relevant option than competitors in the cake industry who take a more general approach to social media advertising.

There is a large amount of data collected about social media platform users; however, not all of this data is useful for developing marketing campaigns. When businesses have access to relevant social media data, they can not only learn more about their customers' activities on social media, but they can also gain deeper insights into how their customers (and potential customers) think, feel, and behave in a variety of scenarios.

## THE INFLUENCE OF SOCIAL MEDIA ON YOUR PROFESSIONAL CAREER

There are millions of people who use social media on a daily basis. In fact, 72 percent of all Internet users use at least one social media platform. The average number of social media accounts is 8.4 per person according to Global Web Index (gwi.com, 2014). Furthermore, social media is no longer just a means of communicating with one's college roommate or grandmother. Individuals, organizations, and businesses from all over the world can view your social media activity. And the people who employ you or are considering hiring you are looking into these things.

Your social media presence is how you present yourself to the rest of the world, which includes both current and future employers. In fact, the impression you give potential employers is frequently formed based on your social media presence. Social media can help you land an interview, improve your chances of getting hired, or even advance you in your current career.

Is your use of social media hurting your chances of getting a job, or is it actually helping you get the job you want? Let us go through it in greater depth.

## ARE YOUR EMPLOYERS CONCERNED ABOUT YOUR SOCIAL MEDIA ACTIVITIES?

You spend a significant amount of time on social media platforms looking up old pictures and posts shared by your friends. Do you think employers have time to sift through social media for potential employees and candidates? Indeed, they do and already are. The use of social media platforms such as Twitter, Facebook, and Instagram is becoming an increasingly important component of hiring and employment decisions made by human resource managers and employers. According to CareerBuilder survey, 70 percent of employers screen potential candidates using their social media accounts (CareerBuilder Hiring Solutions, 2018). This figure will only rise if the current rate of use of social media platforms continues.

There is some good news here, even if you have already stopped reading and are deleting all of your college photos from Facebook. Employers use of social media in the hiring process poses a risk for job seekers, but also an opportunity to differentiate themselves from the competition.

Before you start thinking about how you can use social media to land your next job, make sure your presence on social media isn't inadvertently harming your career.

## PUTTING YOURSELF FORWARD AS A PROFESSIONAL

Unless you're posting it on LinkedIn, your social media profile doesn't need to be as polished as your resume. However, it must remain professional.

You should avoid posting anything that might turn off potential employers or hiring managers. Racist, sexist, or otherwise discriminatory comments are prohibited, as are references to drugs or alcohol, lewd posts or photos, and negative comments about current or former employers. A good rule of thumb to follow here is that if you need clarification before posting something, you shouldn't.

Examine each of your profiles carefully to see if there is any content that should be removed. Also, remember to go way, way back. Many of us have kept the same social media profiles for years, and you probably don't want prospective employers to think of you in the same way that your high school classmates did. Consider the posts and pictures you comment on and like, as these can be displayed on your profile and influence how other people perceive you. Ensure that any content you do not want discovered is removed, untagged, or hidden from view. It is worth the time learning how to take these actions to clean up your profile.

## MAKING USE OF THE PRIVACY SETTINGS ON YOUR SOCIAL MEDIA ACCOUNTS

So, you've gone through all of your social media profiles and removed anything potentially offensive. So, what should we do now? Given your privacy settings, you have complete control over what information potential employers can access. According to a reliable source, 13 million Facebook users have never changed their privacy settings, which may appear to be a ridiculous statistic given how obvious it is.

You should adjust your privacy settings on social media platforms that you primarily use for personal interactions, such as Facebook, so that only those close to you can see your posts, uploads, and photos that you have tagged. However, keep in mind that if you work (or hope to work) in a creative industry like entertainment, your potential employers may want to see your personality on social media. Locking down your privacy settings may have an adverse effect on your chances of getting hired.

## USING SOCIAL MEDIA TO YOUR ADVANTAGE

The potentially negative effects of using social media on one's ability to find gainful employment have recently received a lot of attention. However, there are times when social media can be beneficial. Another survey found that nearly one-third of employers hired an applicant based on something positive they saw on the applicant's social media profile. So, what should you do? You should, as previously stated, clean up your profile. Then, when looking for work, you should use social media in innovative ways to distinguish yourself from other candidates.

Employers can gain a different perspective on a candidate by reviewing their social media profiles.

You can even use social media to highlight qualities that don't necessarily show up on a resume if you use it correctly. Use your various social media profiles to highlight your unique personality, sense of humor, and/or charitable nature. Post photos of yourself running a 5k or helping with a Habitat for Humanity build, as well as (politically correct) jokes, musings on culture or current events, and humorous observations on the world around you. After all, companies want to fill open positions with real people they can work with, not robotic social media accounts designed to give the impression of extreme professionalism.

Even if your actions on social media do not make you appear to be a saint or qualify you for the next Nobel Prize, you can still use your social profiles to demonstrate that you are a well-rounded and interesting person by highlighting the various aspects of your life. If you enjoy the game of chess so much that you spend hours playing it, share your enthusiasm with others by posting chess-related content. Your potential employer will notice your enthusiasm for the role (this is just one example), as well as your ability to think critically and make decisions based on the information you have gathered. If you enjoy knitting and have made scarves, hats, and tea cozies for yourself, use a social platform to showcase your creative endeavors.

It is essential that you use social media in the way that it was intended: to connect, network, and converse with people who share your interests and values. On Twitter, follow the most influential people in your field. Distribute information about the industry or company you want to work for. Making connections, starting conversations, and getting your name out there will go a long way toward distinguishing yourself from the other individuals in your field of competition.

# Chapter Summary

As you can see, social media is much more than just connecting with friends and family and watching funny viral videos. It is a driving force that is changing society and how we interact and connect with one another. But it has also become a place where any or all members of the public, including potential employers, can critically observe and see everything we do. As a result, the very concept of privacy is being questioned.

There are numerous benefits to using social media. We can use it to learn new skills and establish ourself as an authority, demonstrate empathy, kindness, and social awareness, to name a few. Businesses can use it to attract new customers and keep current ones.

However, these engaging platforms contribute to habit-changing patterns by providing us with a steady daily dose of content that is so addictive that we can spend hours on them without realizing it.

Thousands of data points are collected on us while we surf and browse in order to create the ultimate profile for advertisers, based on behavioral data, engagement data, personal data, attitude data, and preference data. Such user characteristics have become so valuable that business marketers can create hyper-targeted marketing campaigns to very specific target audiences, down to their specific needs and desires.

It should go without saying that social media is here to stay. So, we should learn to use it for our benefit. One significant benefit of using social media is that you can use it to further your professional goals as well as make personal connections. You may see significant results if you give your actions and social media presence some thought. Being social could even propel you to the next level of professional success.

## Digital Gold Nuggets

◆ *Make sure that any content you don't want discovered online is removed, untagged, or hidden.*

◆ *Go to Google and type in Google My Activity to get a detailed historical view of your online activity as tracked by Google. You can manage your privacy and security settings and control which data is saved to your account. You can also turn OFF the Ad personalization setting.*

◆ *You have complete control over what information potential employers can access, thanks to your privacy settings.*

◆ *You should change your privacy settings on social media platforms where you primarily interact with people for personal communication.*

# Chapter Eleven

# METAVERSE

The metaverse is a three-dimensional, persistent online world that connects various virtual spaces. It could be compared to a futuristic version of the Internet. Because of the metaverse virtual world, users will be able to collaborate, meet up, play games, shop, and communicate in these 3D settings.

Although the metaverse as a whole is not yet fully developed, there are metaverse-like aspects on various platforms. At the moment, online video games offer the best example of the metaverse experience available. Developers have pushed the boundaries of what a game can be by staging in-game events where users interact with each other.

A metaverse, in other words, is an inclusive digital world that encourages online interaction with other users or platforms. For example, instead of simply talking to a friend via voice call or text, you can converse with them while taking a walk or having coffee in a virtual cafe using your digital avatars (a graphical likeness of yourself). Furthermore, the metaverse opens the door to novel marketing and advertising approaches, thus creating virtual economies.

Consider a user who only ever visits first-person shooter (FPS) gaming communities while in a virtual world. The virtual world can use this information to display advertisements or virtual banners for a new first-person shooter game released by a game studio. All types of goods and services have the same level of practicability.

Many well-known brands have begun to advertise their products in these virtual worlds, including Marvel and Hasbro, as well as Balenciaga, Adidas, and Gucci. Businesses may be able to reach more people through these platforms in the not-too-distant future than they could through traditional marketing methods.

Why? Let's take a closer look. Toys for children are manufactured by companies such as Roblox and Hasbro, among others. Although the majority of customers are the children's parents; it is the responsibility of the children to persuade their parents to buy the products. Children do not always use social media and do not go out as much as adults. This was especially true during the COVID-19 pandemic, when many children attended online school from the comfort of their own homes. Because of the metaverse, businesses will be able to communicate with children who spend their free time playing video games in online worlds.

The Sandbox company is a great example of a digital world based on the concept of property and real estate ownership. On this website platform, businesses will buy "digital land" to display banner ads and advertisements. What exactly is its relationship to your data? It will be impossible to target specific users or create a target audience without using user data.

## DATA AND THE METAVERSE

To appreciate how data will be used in the metaverse, it is necessary to first better understand what the metaverse is. The goal of this digital environment is to create a virtual or augmented reality for consumers to experience in real time. In virtual worlds, users can work, shop, and entertain themselves in addition to conversing with one another.

Let's take a closer look at the role of data in the metaverse, as well as some current trends:

## THE STANDARDIZATION OF DATA

Consider OpenSea or Binance, two platforms that sell non-fungible tokens (NFTs). NFTs will be discussed in greater detail in the next chapter. Contracts are formed in blockchain networks (also explained later) based on each token that is exchanged, sold, or minted.

Businesses that have access to market data such as trade volumes and floor prices can make more informed decisions about the launch of their new tokens or the user experience associated with these tokens.

## ADVERTISING IN THE METAVERSE

Facebook changed its name to Meta, but the data it accumulated over time could still be used to support Facebook's own metaverse. There will undoubtedly be new users, but there will also be a significant number of previous Facebook platform users who will have direct access to the upcoming metaverse. In addition to their identities, Meta's digital world will include marketing data associated with those identities. Advertisers and businesses can use this data to market their wares in the digital world, which can be used by both the user and the marketer.

The Sandbox company, a decentralized, community-driven platform where creators can create voxel assets (or collectable entities) and gaming experiences and monetize them on the blockchain, now has over 500,000 members, each of whom can create their own games and in-world materials. If an advertiser could successfully handle all of the data available from this entire population of consumers, marketing campaigns could be greatly improved by segmenting distinct groups. Similarly, data gathered from external sources can be used to promote specific tokens or attributes to users based on the interests expressed by those users.

## CAPABILITIES IN NETWORK AND DATA ENGINEERING

Metaverse expansion and innovation will continue at a rapid pace. By 2032, the addition of metaverses is expected to account for a 20-fold increase in the amount of data we consume (Credit Suisse, 2022). As a result, more cutting-edge data solutions will be required to effectively deal with these massive amounts of data exchanges.

Businesses will find it extremely difficult to catch up if they do not prepare for the processing and utilization of this data. The volume of data generated will have increased dramatically, and the flow of data generated will be extremely dense. Data platforms must be equipped to deal with this data in order for business owners to be able to acquire and analyze this data.

There could be a number of impediments, such as an excessive number of data sources and segmented data. However, if they start right away, they will undoubtedly be able to benefit from the metaverse.

# Chapter Summary

According to Facebook, the future is here, as this technology behemoth took the bold step of changing its name to Meta and spent more than 10 billion rebranding and repositioning itself for the future in an immersive virtual world. In addition, many well-known brands have already established a presence in the metaverse by copywriting their brands, selling their products, and purchasing "digital land" in the metaverse.

This 3D version of the Internet will undoubtedly create an unpresented number of new opportunities for advertisers, entertainers, creators and businesses in this new digital world. As a result, the global economic impact will skyrocket to unprecedented heights.

Data and artificial intelligence (AI) are critical aspects of the metaverse, and companies with the most data and the ability to process such data to drive insights, and to reach the audience for their advertisers and online consumers, will have the most advantage in this new digital world.

However, given the nature of the digital footprint and the sheer number of users expected to be online and engaged, the metaverse will exponentially increase the amount of data available as well as the challenges to effectively deal with it.

## Digital Gold Nuggets

◆ *The goal of this digital environment is to create a virtual or augmented reality for consumers to experience in real time. In virtual worlds, users can work, shop, and entertain themselves in addition to conversing with one another.*

◆ *Do some research about the metaverse and explore opportunities that the metaverse presents.*

◆ *Have fun and create your avatar that you would like to see in the metaverse. There are a number of mobile apps that allow you to do this.*

# Chapter Twelve

NFTs AND BLOCKCHAIN

I t seems like everyone is excited about a new technological breakthrough known as NFTs (non-fungible tokens). We will look at the rapid growth of NFTs in this chapter. It is no secret that this new industry has enormous growth potential. NFTs are data units stored on the blockchain network. So real assets, such as paintings, music files, or digital art, are represented by the token. In fact, NFTs provide a certificate of authenticity or ownership of the particular asset.

They enable anyone to obtain an original item based on a contract stored on the blockchain. As a result, the barriers to stealing, copying, or producing fakes are removed.

Blockchain technology is a digitally distributed, decentralized computer network that uses a method of recording information that makes changing, hacking, or manipulating the system impossible or difficult. A blockchain is a distributed ledger that duplicates and distributes transactions across the network of computers that comprise the blockchain.

The structure of data differs greatly between a traditional database and a blockchain. A blockchain stores information in groups known as blocks, which contain data sets.

The blockchain is being combined with artificial intelligence (AI) by developers in the technology innovation sector to improve the efficiency of smart contracts used to generate NFTs. As they currently stand, NFT smart contracts are self-executing in the sense that they can check for and execute contract terms without the assistance of a third party or a central authority. A smart contract is essentially a mechanism for carrying out a purchase agreement between the owner of the NFT and the buyer.

This breakthrough technology has the potential to democratize the creative economy by allowing artists to communicate directly with the general public. Despite the fact that NFTs are gaining popularity around the world due to transactions involving millions of dollars and the tokens' potential, there is still a great deal of obscurity surrounding the procedure by which these tokens are generated.

How do distributed ledger technologies such as blockchain and artificial intelligence function behind the scenes, and what role do they play in the overall process? Let's see if we can help you find answers to these questions by looking at some of the cutting-edge work being done in the fields of NFTs and AI.

Initially, NFT artwork was created by human artists. However, a significant amount of time and energy has recently been invested in teaching artificial intelligence to create original works of art on its own. While the majority of digital NFT artworks currently available on the Internet were created by utilizing randomly generated characteristics within a JPEG (standard compressed image file) format, true AI artwork would have a significantly higher level of variation and creativity than what is currently available in the NFT marketplace. Because of the ability to create one-of-a-kind works of art in real time, this presents a potentially lucrative opportunity for prospective future NFT minters.

Eponym, an artificial intelligence (AI) software that can transform text into pictures that resemble works of art, was recently launched and allows artists to sell their work directly on the NFT marketplace OpenSea. The blockchain now provides public access to the artwork created with Eponym. Eponym, unlike other types of AI-based art, is not entirely reliant on AI algorithms, allowing for human intervention.

You're probably wondering how the general public is exposed to this type of artwork at this point. There are now AI-powered art galleries that allow artists to connect with people who might buy their work. Art AI is one of the most well-known artificial intelligence art galleries. I believe that the true value of AI in the NFT market will manifest as a more intelligent and adaptable method of market management. An artificial intelligence capable of detecting trends in the NFT marketplace and making real-time adjustments to prices, listings, and other market factors will be useful for any online store, but it will be especially useful for an emerging market like NFTs. It will be easier for new customers to join the fold and become investors if the purchasing process is streamlined and personalized. Some businesses have created a one-of-a-kind ticketing experience for their customers that is entirely based on blockchain technology.

These tickets are distributed in the form of NFTs, and users can choose to airdrop them and keep them as collectibles in addition to using them for events hosted in the metaverse.

The possibilities for NFTs are practically limitless, as evidenced by the accomplishments that have already been made in this sector. For example, thanks to a brand-new OpenAI project, anyone will soon be able to generate an infinite number of high-quality computer-generated NFTs by simply typing in a line of text. DALL-E 2, the technology driving this innovation, is an artificial intelligence picture generator named after Salvador Dali and WALL-E. It accomplishes this by combining GPT-3, OpenAI's natural language processor, with over 650 million Internet-sourced photos. This is how it achieves such amazing results. MetaScapes is another AI-powered software that combines images to create new visuals.

The MetaScape is made up of two parts: a generator, which is in charge of producing an output, and a discriminator, which analyzes the generator's operations and gives it instructions on how to improve the output. To use MetaScape, users upload images with descriptive labels attached in order to use the software. Following that, the AI computer examines the photos and labels associated with them to generate new images that are a synthesis of the previous ones.

There are numerous other examples of innovations in the same vein where AI is giving NFT technology an advantage. With the help of the NFT project Fuzzle, the concept of digital companionship is taken to new heights. Endless AI and Gala Games, a massive blockchain gaming company, collaborated to create Fuzzle. It is presented as unique and ownable non-fungible tokens (NFTs), which are far more useful than the tiny keychain pets from the 1990s. In those early days, NFTs were manually printed and used as small decorative items, often worn by the owner.

Fuzzles are created to interact with one another in a friendly, human-like manner. They are also emotionally sensitive and understand human emotions. It is said that they can give wise advice or even take action to make you feel better when you are down.

As evidenced by the types of innovations and approaches taken, AI and NFT have collaborated to create truly unique experiences and have made many previously unimaginable opportunities available to everyone. The NFT market is still in its early stages, and much of its potential has yet to be realized. As we move forward, there is one thing we can be certain of: This technology will be one that radically changes how we own things, and the world will witness some incredible innovations in this space as a result.

# Chapter Summary

The world of NFTs and Blockchain is extremely exciting because it introduces many new ways and opportunities to view and manage the world of digital art and the thriving online creative industry.

Consider the advantages to creative rights, copyrights, and digital ownership. Because of the lack of controls over digital properties, these have come under attack in the digital realm.

NFTs, on the other hand, will allow greater controls and economic opportunities for the artist and creator. All of this is made possible by data and artificial intelligence.

Although NFTs have a lot of potential, they also have a lot of risks because of their early-stage adoption and a lack of regulations, structure, and uniformity. However, the future looks promising for the various applications and opportunities presented by this new technology.

## Digital Gold Nuggets

♦ *NFTs enable anyone to obtain an original item based on a contract stored on the blockchain. As a result, the barriers to stealing, copying, or producing fakes are removed.*

♦ *Consider the new creative and economic opportunities made available by NFTs and the Blockchain platform for your creative and original artwork if you are an artist.*

# Chapter Thirteen

## WEB 1.0 – 3.0 AND THE DARK WEB

The World Wide Web was designed with a "hyperlinked information system" in mind. In essence, it is an on-screen data library that can be accessed by clicking on text or images, as you do now. The purpose of the Internet hasn't changed much over the years, but how we use it, how businesses and consumers interact with it, and the technology that powers it have. This chapter will go over the monumental transition from Web 1.0 to 3.0 and will take a look at the mysterious Dark Web.

### WEB 1.0 IS ALSO REFERRED TO AS "THE INTERNET"

The Internet as we know it evolved from what is now known as the "read-only web." Websites' sole purpose was to provide information, and they only contained evergreen content. The website's pages were only linked to one another via hyperlinks, and there was no interactive content or design elements.

## THE FIRST VERSIONS OF SEARCH ENGINES

The "Archie Query Form" was the world's very first search engine. Lycos, which was founded in 1994, quickly became one of the most popular and successful search engines (who else, except me, had an email address that ended in.lycos?). The following year saw the launch of AltaVista, which reached its peak usage of 80 million users per day in 1996. This is a staggering number for such a short period of time. Yahoo, one of the few search engines to launch in the 1990s and survive Google's dominance, began operations in 1995 and continues to operate today.

When Larry Page and Sergey Brin founded Google, they were working on a school project at Stanford University and had a vision of a search engine that analyzed web pages based on how many times a search term appeared on the page. Google did not begin operations until three years later, in 1998. Isn't it incredible how things have changed?

Web 1.0 is the first stage of the World Wide Web's evolution. In Web 1.0, the majority of users were content consumers, with only a few exceptions being content creators. Static pages hosted on web servers owned by ISPs (Internet Service Providers) or free web hosting services were commonplace.

In other words, Web 1.0 was designed to make it easier for people to find information online. This version of the web was designed for people looking for information. It is sometimes referred to as the "read-only web" because it lacks the forms, visuals, controls, and interactivity that we have come to expect from the modern Internet.

People coined the term "Web 1.0" to describe the first version of the Internet. Users were able to see a glimpse of the future of digital communication and information-sharing possibilities as a result.

Web 1.0 had several distinguishing characteristics, including:

- Static pages were linked to a computer system via hyperlinks
- The data was stored in a filesystem on the server rather than a relational database management system, so HTML (Hypertext Markup Language) forms were delivered via e-mail
- A variety of graphics were included

Digitize a real-world dictionary and make it available online to anyone who needs a quick reference but can't react to it, and you've got Web 1.0!

## WEB 2.0 - THE PRESENT

Web 2.0, in contrast to the original Web 1.0, consists of a much larger number of people creating content for a much larger audience. Web 2.0 is all about contributing and participating, whereas Web 1.0 was all about reading and navigating.

This version of the Internet emphasizes UGC (user-generated content), ease of use, interactivity, and improved system and device compatibility. The end user's experience is central to Web 2.0. As a result of this Web form, communities, collaborations, dialogues, and social media were formed. Consequently, the vast majority of today's Internet users primarily communicate via Web 2.0.

Web 2.0 is also known as "the participatory social Web," as opposed to the "read-only Web." Web 2.0 is an improved and more powerful version of Web 1.0, made possible by the addition of JavaScript frameworks (collection of libraries containing code written in JavaScript) and other new features in web browsers.

The following are some common Web 2.0 characteristics:

- It offers free data sorting, allowing users to collectively retrieve and categorize information.
- It displays dynamic content in response to user searches.
- Users can interact in a variety of ways, including self-use and collaboration.
- The term "social media" can refer to;
    ◊ Tagging
    ◊ Blogging
    ◊ Commenting
    ◊ Using RSS (Really Simple Syndication) as a way to make news, blogs and other content available to subscribers
    ◊ On-line Networking
    ◊ Voting on web content

- It is used by society as a whole, not just a few niche groups.
- The rise of mobile Internet access and social networks has aided Web 2.0's growth. This growth is also being fueled by mobile devices such as Android-powered smartphones and Apple's iPhones. As a result of Web 2.0's growth, apps such as Facebook, Instagram, Pinterest, TikTok, Twitter, and YouTube, to name a few, were able to grow and dominate the online landscape.

## THE FUTURE OF WEB 3.0

Finally, we arrive at the most recent Web version. To fully comprehend the significance of Web 3.0, we must look to the future. Despite the fact that some of its components are already available, Web 3.0 will take some time to be fully realized. Web 2.0 is a "participative social Web," while Web 3.0 is a "read, write, and execute Web."

In Web 3.0 users will move away from centralized platforms, like Facebook or Google, and toward decentralized, almost anonymous platforms at this stage of web use. Tim Berners-Lee coined the phrase "Web 3.0" to describe an Internet that could potentially process content conceptually and contextually using artificial intelligence (AI) and machine learning (ML).

However, this idealized version of the Web has not come to fruition to date due to technological constraints such as high development cost and difficulty of converting human language into a form that computers can understand.

Web 3.0 features conceptually include the following:

- A Semantic Web, in which search and analysis will be used to help users create, share, and connect content. It consists of a common framework to make Internet data machine-readable.
- The system will employ both machine learning and artificial intelligence (AI). Natural Language Processing (NLP) can be used to create a computer that can better understand and respond to its users' needs.
- The "Internet of Things" (IoT), which refers to the interconnectedness of various devices and applications. This process is enabled by semantic metadata which describes the meanings of values and the names of data components. They will make it possible to connect to the Internet without a computer or smartphone at all times.
- It will be a "trustless" service because it allows users to communicate publicly or privately without fear of their data being compromised by a third party.
- Graphics will be rendered in three dimensions. This can already be seen in computer games, virtual reality tours, and e-commerce.
- Participation will be enabled without the need for approval from a governing body.

Web 3.0 can be useful in the following applications:

- Metaverses: An infinite virtual world built with 3D modelling and rendering technology.
- Blockchain games that adhere to the principles of NFTs, allowing players to have actual ownership of in-game resources.

- Digital infrastructure and personal information security.
- More secure personal information as part of decentralized financial transactions.
- Universal Digital Payment Gateway.
- Blockchain-based autonomous organizations, peer-to-peer digital financial transactions, smart contracts, and cryptocurrency transactions.
- Members of online communities owning the sites.

Keep in mind that Web 3.0 has not yet been implemented. The Augmented Reality (AR) Cloud, a technology used to create immersive experiences, as well as other Web 3.0 elements like NFTs, Blockchain, and distributed ledgers are already infiltrating our online experiences. Siri and the Internet of Things (IoT) are also Web 3.0 technologies which are already in existence. When Web 3.0 is fully implemented, it will be closer to Berners Lee's original vision of an Internet that can process content conceptually. There will be "no single point of failure" because you will not need permission from any "central authority" to post anything. There will also be no "kill switch."

Despite this, there is still much work to be done, particularly in speech recognition, because human speech contains a dizzying array of nuances and terms that technology cannot yet fully comprehend. It's come a long way, but the process is still far from complete.

## THE DARK WEB

The dark web is often depicted as a mysterious and hard-to-understand part of the Internet, so let's bust that myth.

Since it was made available to the general public for the first time in the 1990s, the Internet has undergone a variety of transformations, one of the most contentious of which is the expansion of what is known as the "dark web."

The dark web may worry some adults, especially since media reports frequently associate it with risky or illegal online activity. The dark web does have some positive aspects, though; because, as with everything else online, issues are more often brought on by how people use technology than by the technology itself. To assist you in gaining a deeper comprehension of the dark web, the following is a comparison of three distinct kinds of webs:

## OPEN WEB

This refers to the part of the Internet that is accessible to the general public and can be accessed by using a search engine such as Google or Bing. The majority of people use this part of the Internet on a daily basis.

## DEEP WEB

This is the portion of the Internet that is typically concealed from the view of the general public. It is not possible to access it through typical search engines; rather, it can be reached through other, less well-known, methods.

The vast majority of what is referred to as the "deep web" consists of databases that can be accessed in a safe manner via the "open web." Examples of such databases include those pertaining to online hotel reservations, online shopping, medical records, banking, and similar activities. Password protection ensures that the content can be accessed only by those who have been granted permission to do so (for example, employees).

## DARK WEB

The vast majority of Internet users connect to the Internet using a personal computer or other electronic device that permits the user to be assigned a distinct Internet Protocol (IP) address. This address serves as the user user's online identity.

With the help of an IP address, networks are able to deliver the appropriate data to the appropriate location, such as ensuring that an email is delivered to its intended recipient. Using a person's unique IP address, it is possible to track and monitor all of their activity on the Internet. However, in the dark web a person can browse the internet anonymously.

It is very challenging to determine which websites a user has visited because the dark web uses sophisticated systems to anonymize a user's real IP address. Anonymous access to it is typically granted through the use of specialized software, of which Tor (The Onion Router) is the most well-known.

Over 2 million people use Tor on a daily basis (Users – Tor Metrics, n.d.). Tor is a method that allows users to browse both the open web and the dark web anonymously, without anyone being able to identify them or monitor their activity.

The vast majority of the websites can be found on the deep web, and many of these sites are operated by organizations such as businesses, government agencies, financial institution and charitable organizations. Within the realm of the deep web is a section of the Internet referred to as the dark web. This section of the Internet is inaccessible to users who do not have the Tor browser installed on their devices. Even though it is perfectly legal to use Tor, the vast majority of regular Internet users will never have a need to access any content that is located on the dark web.

The deep web and the dark web seem to be pretty interchangeable terms, but what exactly sets them apart?

Every day, millions of people who use the Internet regularly log into their personal databases, such as their email inboxes and credit card accounts. On the deep web, these pages are secured by security walls, authentication forms, and passwords and are not indexed by search engines.

## HOW EXACTLY DOES TOR OPERATE?

As noted above, Tor is a software that allows people to access the dark web. Tor provides anonymization and can be accessed through a search engine, after which it can be downloaded at no cost. The sender's message is encapsulated in multiple layers of encryption using the Tor network. These layers are reminiscent of the layers of an onion. This concept is what gives Tor its name (i.e. The Onion Router, abbreviated to "Tor").

When using the Tor browser, searches and messages do not arrive at their final destination in the same way that they were sent. They are instead transmitted by means of "nodes," which are other computers that are operated by Tor users. Following the removal of one layer of encryption at each node in the chain, the message is then passed on to the subsequent node in the chain. Every node in the chain is aware of the identity of the node that came before it and the node that comes after it, but they are unaware of the identities of the nodes that are further along or further before. As a result, it is extremely challenging to follow the path of a message throughout its entire journey, let alone determine where it originated or who sent it.

## WHEN AND WHY EXACTLY DID THE DARK WEB COME INTO EXISTENCE?

The release of Freenet in the year 2000 is credited with marking the beginning of the dark web. Freenet was the thesis project of Ian Clarke, a student at the University of Edinburgh. Clarke's goal was to develop an anonymous "Distributed Decentralized Information Storage and Retrieval System." The objective of Clarke's project was to develop a novel approach to anonymous online communication and file sharing. This groundwork served as the foundation for the Tor Project, which was initially released in 2002 with the subsequent release of a browser in 2008. Tor enabled users to surf the Internet in complete anonymity, including website that were previously considered inaccessible as part of the dark web.

## UTILIZATIONS OF THE DARK WEB THAT ARE LEGAL

Despite the fact that utilizing the dark web may appear questionable at first glance, doing so is entirely within the law, and there are many valid applications for anonymous browsing with Tor. As an illustration, the dark web is frequently used as a means of communication in countries where government surveillance can be used to spy on and oppress political dissidents. Even with these additional layers of protection, users should still exercise caution when navigating the dark web and implement appropriate safety precautions. These precautions include avoiding the use of standard email addresses, browsing with a powerful virtual private network (VPN), and performing periodic security software updates, all of which can compromise the secrecy of the dark web.

## ILLICIT ACTIVITIES CONDUCTED THROUGH THE DARK WEB

Due to the fact that it is anonymous, the dark web is sometimes used for nefarious and even unlawful purposes. Trading in illegal pornography and other potentially harmful materials, as well as buying and selling illegal drugs, weapons, passwords, and identities that have been stolen, are all examples of these types of negative activities. Silk Road, AlphaBay, and Hansa are just a few examples of the websites that hosted illegal content that were uncovered by government agencies in recent years and shut down as a result. The anonymity of the dark web has, over the course of the last few decades, been a contributing factor in the proliferation of various cybersecurity threats and data breaches.

## HOW RISKY IS IT TO BROWSE THE DARK WEB?

When you are careless about what content you access on the dark web, you put yourself in jeopardy. You run the risk of unwittingly disclosing personal information to cybercriminals and may even do so unintentionally. You might also find yourself involved in illegal activity without even being aware of it. Because there is such a high volume of illegal activity and the possibility that you will find content that is extremely upsetting, there is also the risk of suffering mental trauma. If you decide to venture into the dark web, you should keep these concerns in mind, particularly if you are not technically savvy.

The dark web is frequently associated with illegal or dangerous online activity. Tor is software that provides anonymity and is accessible via a search engine. It enables users to browse the open and dark webs anonymously, without allowing anyone to identify or monitor their activity. Tor's anonymity allowed users to surf the dark web completely anonymously and access websites that were previously considered to be part of the "dark web."

Users should still exercise caution and take appropriate safety precautions when navigating the dark web. The dark web is frequently used for illegal activities such as illegal drugs, weapons, passwords, and stolen identities. In recent years, the anonymity of the dark web has contributed to cybersecurity threats and data breaches.

Despite this, there are many people who choose to use the dark web for legitimate reasons. Political dissidents and individuals who wish to keep certain information private are two examples of these people.

# Chapter Summary

So, while the dark web looms in the background, the Internet has progressed from its humble beginnings as a "read-only web" and a simple search of an online dictionary to today's highly interactive, socially engaging, data-rich, and visually appealing content provided by a global community of creators, and expected to evolve eventually to a 3D interactive model, likely powered by Artificial Intelligence (AI) and Machine Learning (ML).

In a nutshell, we've progressed from "read-only web" to "participative social web," with Web 3.0 on the horizon as a conceptual and contextual "read, write, and execute web" where everything will be connected.

In addition, we now know that very sophisticated systems and specialized software are used to mask and grant access to limited data within the realm of the deep web known as the dark web. Nonetheless, it is legitimately used by certain people, institutions and governments.

Despite the negative aspects associated with the notorious dark web, where negative consequences are often caused by how people use technology rather than by the technology itself, the Internet continues to thrive and expand its acceptance among the global population.

This is innovation at its finest, as the world community has come together in one place in less than a generation to create, innovate, communicate, socialize, and share with one another, while blurring the lines of time-zones and the world's borders.

Given what we've accomplished in such a short period of time, the future appears very promising; however, the unknown or what could go wrong is unsettling.

## Digital Gold Nuggets

♦ *When you are careless about what content you access on the dark web, you put yourself in jeopardy. You run the risk of unwittingly disclosing personal information to cybercriminals and may even do so unintentionally.*

♦ *The future appears to be bright. Continue to observe and learn about our rapidly changing world as a result of technology, as well as global trends related to it, to see how you can benefit or leverage it.*

# CONCLUSION

decided to write this book because of the amount of change that technology and innovation have brought about in our society in just one generation.

I didn't want us to forget how far we've come in such a short period of time, and how the PC and microchip revolutions sparked the changes that propelled us forward from their humble beginnings.

Data is now the most valuable commodity of the future, supporting much of the innovation. In fact, it appears to be like gold.

We've seen how data has evolved into the fuel that drives many businesses' goals and engines. Based on our searches, behavioral habits, and purchasing patterns, we've seen how it's collected, measured, analyzed, and used for marketers and advertisers.

Nothing compares to what the world is witnessing and experiencing as a result of the digital revolution, the Internet as the information highway, and the ease of access across all industries and sectors of societies around the world.

New business models have emerged to meet our every need and convenience online as a result of widespread acceptance of the Internet, booming mobile device usage, and vast amounts of data.

## WHAT WE'VE LEARNED

Data is the new gold. It has surpassed oil as the world's most valuable commodity, and it will continue to power everything we do online.

As a result of the digital revolution and the proliferation of device connectivity and online users, we are rapidly approaching an insurmountable stockpile of data that will be incomprehensible and impossible to process without the assistance of AI and ML.

AI and ML enhanced processing of data will notably aid in improving quality of life, making better decisions, and producing the best results. Manufacturing and automation, medical and healthcare, banking and finance, science, insurance, education, and recreation, as well as customer experience and problem resolution, will all benefit from the use of AI and ML.

AI and ML will also aid in the delivery of innovations such as self-driving cars and robotics, as well as the improvement and innovation of sports and sporting experiences.

Although we concluded that Information is power, it is only power for the few people who have access to it. The "digital divide" describes how socioeconomic, gender prejudice, and cultural divides, as well as a country's infrastructure, economic, and development status, are expanding social and economic gaps globally. It is also defined as the ability to keep pace with the shift in how technology is used and accessed, as well as staying current with new innovations.

For countries to avoid falling behind, their governments and institutions must, wherever possible, lead the way by investing in and making technology available across the countries entire population, rather than focusing on incremental innovation that results in positive change for only limited sectors of their country.

We discovered how online data collection and harvesting are causing unimaginable amounts of data to be generated. Although, there are many ways to collect data, it is becoming clear that data for data exchanged online is the simplest and most effective means of leveraging our digital power, because we give our data every time we go online or use a technology device that can track our activities and movements. Data is only valuable when it can be converted into insights and used to train AI through ML to produce powerful algorithms that drive results and efficient decision making.

We investigated the concept of privacy and discovered that it has all but vanished or is constantly under attack, particularly because we leave a digital footprint almost everywhere we go online, unknowingly providing a digital inventory that can be used to profit from our identity.

Furthermore, service providers and platforms may store cookies (tracking codes) on our computers or device, and advertisers may use some of these saved cookies to present us with a recommended purchase based on our most recent search or interest.

The good news is that privacy policies are still in place, and remain a priority for Big Tech companies. As a result, many user control settings are available on their platforms and devices for us to set up, change, or implement to help keep our data secure. In addition, by installing a VPN (Virtual Private Network), we can further protect our data.

As we look to the future, we see that AI will drive efficiency and productivity in the new economy. Furthermore, the future will be driven by innovation and creativity, with a virtual world somewhat mimicking the activities of the natural world as we know it, potentially evolving as a result of AI.

The spread of digital innovation will benefit the economy by impacting various industries and generating new revenue streams, as well as providing significant improvements in labor productivity and creating a new virtual workforce.

Today, AI is the logical way forward given the vast amount of data available and the projected explosive growth of data in the future. However, our reliance on AI may change our world in ways we never imagined or anticipated.

With the United States and Asia emerging as global leaders, many countries may fall further behind in the use of technology, resulting in an even larger economic gap than we currently have.

There is varying perspective by futurist and experts on the future impact of AI on the new economy: It could result in rapid expansion of the economy, transforming our society in almost every area, and we humans will need to make the most adjustments. Alternatively change may only apply in certain sectors for a long time to come.

We also looked at social media and acknowledged that it is a powerful tool for connecting and interacting with people all over the world. It allows us to interact online more efficiently, form connections, and acquire and disseminate information more quickly than ever before.

Many people are using social media to raise awareness about a cause that is important to them within a larger audience than they would otherwise have access to. Businesses can also use social media to promote their products and services. It is proving to be a great place for businesses to increase brand awareness, get instant feedback, and grow their market through advertisement and engagement. This is a result of the hyper-targeting opportunities provided by these platforms and algorithms to help them connect with those ideal customers.

However, given social media's apparent addictive nature and our ability to become lost while browsing endless content, we must exercise caution and limit the amount of time we spend on it. We should also change the notification settings and privacy controls to protect our personal information and to limit our consumption.

Because of social media, our society appears to be rating and judging one another based on the image we project online. Strangers, potential employers, government officials, and law enforcement, as well as friends, are starting to use it to assess others. This type of peer evaluation could lead to the development of a "new social scoring" system, similar to the one used by the shared ride and lodging industries, Uber, and Air BnB. The Netflix Twilight Zone "Nosedive" episode and the film "In Time" are two examples of how this could work in the future. There is technology that already exists that allows us to track, rate, and rank one another solely based on our online profiles. The degree of social stratification is likely to increase even more if we get to the point where a "social credit" system determines a person's social standing. The disparity between those with high ratings and those with low ratings will widen over time. That's when we will start sliding down the slippery slope of digital discrimination.

The significance and pervasiveness of your personal data cannot be overstated. Because the digital revolution and the fact that our world has gone online, thanks in part to the COVID-19 pandemic, there is no turning back. So, we must take every precaution to protect our data from criminals or those with malicious intent. To avoid becoming a victim or a contributor, you must take all necessary precautions to safeguard your data, such as installing virus protection software on all of your devices and encrypting your data. Take note of your online and social media footprint because you could be providing personal identity information to criminals looking for such unsuspecting innocence. In fact, take a thorough inventory of your online presence to see what personal information is available on social platforms. This will give you a better understanding of what you can control and will provide you with peace of mind. Keep all software and device manufacturer updates up to date at all times.

Following the discovery that your personal data is gold and that it is being collected and harvested for financial gain by online platforms, and that you should do everything in your power to protect it, the opportunity to monetize your very own data has also arisen; that is, to profit from the current data for a cash windfall. As a result, you can have control over how and by whom your data is used. Given that advertisers will pay a premium to get your attention, and digital data brokers are constantly on the lookout for new sources of data due to its value, it only makes sense to do your due diligence to see where you can profit.

Remember that your personal history and digital footprint include previous addresses, phone numbers, school records, employment records, certifications, and criminal histories. E-mails and other text files, photos, videos, music, and other audio recordings are examples of physical electronic items that form part of your digital footprint.

As previously stated, you can make money without doing much work if you don't mind sharing your information. However, do your background checks before you share.

We examined what the new economy might look like given data is the newest commodity, but what about the world's future as it becomes more digital? According to various sources, 70% of the global population is online or uses the Internet. This means that all of those people generate massive amounts of data in the form of digital footprints and activities, not to mention the insights gathered and stored, resulting in massive amounts of data that only AI can sort through and make sense of. As a result, AI will shape the future, permeating all industries and job sectors. Our interaction and daily experience will be very different from what it is today as a result of the implementation of AI algorithms and ML techniques, possibly aided by automation and robotics.

This could, however, create new job opportunities in machine learning, data mining and analysis, AI software development, program management, and testing, to name a few sectors.

We anticipate a higher quality of life and more unique opportunities as a result of AI-directed automation and security, AI-driven work and supporting systems, improved human-computer interaction, and potentially AI-assisted healthcare. However, given the unknowns and uncharted waters of AI, there are still numerous concerns.

As our society progresses down the digital path of social networks and online communities, social media clearly leads the way due to its widespread global usage and growing influence in our daily lives. As a result, social media is undeniably here to stay.

We use it for almost everything, from personal and professional endeavors to simply connecting and interacting with others.

We also established that using social media has numerous advantages. It can be used to gain authority, learn new skills, demonstrate empathy and kindness, for content discovery, and for building social awareness, to name a few. Businesses can use it to both attract new customers and retain existing ones.

By providing us with a consistent daily dose of content that is so addictive that we spend hours on viewing them without realizing it, these engaging platforms, on the other hand, might be contributing to irreversible habit-changing patterns.

Another innovative use of data and AI is the metaverse where data is being used once again to power the development of a possible, soon-to-be-mainstream, virtual world that will immerse the average online user. This new digital world will not only create new lived experiences and economic opportunities, but it will also create opportunities for advertisers, entertainers, creators, and businesses, all of which will be driven by AI and data. Comparable experiences already exist in the gaming and simulation industries.

And of course, we cannot mention innovative Metaverse applications without mentioning the blockchain which is another technology innovation underpinned by data. It is a decentralized network with built-in checks and balances on which AI driven innovative solutions and applications live. NFTs have their inherent digital ownership rights and signature, and are spawning their own AI-driven eco-system.

We've seen how the Web has progressed from Web 1.0 to Web 2.0, and it's now on its way to the future AI-driven Web 3.0, which will be interconnected with everything, while the dark web lurks in the shadows.

In closing this book, we've seen how our personal data has become such a valuable commodity that it has spawned and transformed industries, and how the race for data supremacy is concentrated in the hands of a few tech behemoths.

We've also seen how simple it is to trade our data/ information for convenience, entertainment, and instant gratification, while others collect and harvest it to gain insights into our behavioral psychology, allowing them to develop innovative products and services that not only fuel business growth, but also shape the future of business and society.

Some of these companies provide enticing behavioral and habit-changing services that will result in long-term and irreversible social change.

On a final note, the there are several parallels between Internet shopping in the 1990s and artificial intelligence today: Individuals who took advantage of electronic intermediaries were able to reinvent themselves and thrive in the click-and-mortar world. Others have seen their physical locations fade and appear digitally swapped. Individuals who wait too long to ride the wave of social technological advancement risk commodification or extinction.

So, our journey began with a look at the impact of data and its value as a commodity, as well as the evolution of technological innovations brought about by the PC and microchip to the numerous innovations brought about by the digital revolution and its allure.

Then we looked ahead to the future of business and society, offering some practical steps, including some digital gold nuggets, to help you reclaim and reposition your power. As you can see, data is the new gold, and its value will only increase in the future, especially with the help of artificial intelligence, because they will serve as the fundamental basis of our new world.

# ABOUT THE AUTHOR

Wayne is a technology specialist with over 20 years' experience in the data and analytics field. He is passionate about technological innovations, especially those driven by data, analytics, AI, and their impact on the future of business.

He is the founding Director of 2020 Insight Consulting & Marketing, which provides digital services such as business analytics, insight-driven consulting, and digital marketing to assist businesses in making better business decisions by leveraging their valuable data resources. He is also the founding President of TRUTH Communications Media & Publications.

Wayne spent four years at Toronto Metropolitan University (formerly Ryerson University) completing their bachelor's degree program in computer science. In 2015, he upgraded and broadened his academic portfolio by enrolling in the "Big Data Analytics" program at his alma mater.

For over ten years, he has served on the board of directors of MissionFest Toronto, one of Canada's largest event-based organizations focused on missions. He also served as interim executive director just prior to the COVID-19 pandemic.

# REFERENCES

1. Live, W. P. (2022, July 12). *Transcript: The Path Forward: American Competitiveness with Pat Gelsinger, CEO, Intel*. Washington Post. https://www.washingtonpost.com/washington-post-live/2022/07/12/transcript-path-forward-american-competitiveness-with-pat-gelsinger-ceo-intel/

2. Hardesty, L. (2022, February 14). How AWS scientists help create the NFL's Next Gen Stats. Amazon Science. https://www.amazon.science/latest-news/how-aws-scientists-help-create-the-nfls-next-gen-stats

3. The Economist. (2017, May 11). The world's most valuable resource is no longer oil, but data. Retrieved February 24, 2022, from https://www.economist.com/leaders/2017/05/06/the-worlds-most-valuable-resource-is-no-longer-oil-but-data

4. PWC. (2018) The macroeconomic impact of artificial intelligence. UK: PWC

5. Eustis, J. M. (2013, April). Tech Services on the Web: Steven J. Miller's Metadata Resources Page https://pantherfile.uwm.edu/mll/www/resource.html. Technical Services Quarterly, 30(2), 237–238. https://doi.org/10.1080/07317131.2013.760372

6. THE AI FRONTIER MODELING THE IMPACT OF AI ON THE WORLD ECONOMY. (2018, September). www.mckinsey.com. Retrieved March 5, 2022, from https://www.mckinsey.com/~/media/McKinsey/Featured%20Insights/Artificial%20Intelligence/Notes%20from%20the%20frontier%20

Modeling%20the%20impact%20of%20AI%20on%20the%20
world%20economy/MGI-Notes-from-the-AI-frontier-Modeling-
the-impact-of-AI-on-the-world-economy-September-2018.ashx

7.   International Telecommunication Union (ITU). (2020). The
     gender digital divide. https://www.itu.int.

8.   World Bank Group. (2018, November 21). Connecting for
     Inclusion: Broadband Access for All. World Bank. Retrieved
     March 8, 2022, from https://www.worldbank.org/en/topic/
     digitaldevelopment/brief/connecting-for-inclusion-broadband-
     access-for-all

9.   Facts and figures 2021. (2021, November 15). Retrieved
     March 8, 2022, from https://www.itu.int/itu-d/reports/
     statistics/2021/11/15/the-gender-digital-divide/

10.  Burgess, M. (2022, January 27). Google Has a New Plan to
     Kill Cookies. People Are Still Mad. WIRED. Retrieved March 8,
     2022, from https://www.wired.com/story/google-floc-cookies-
     chrome-topics/

11.  The History of Artificial Intelligence. (2017, August 28).
     Science in the News. Retrieved February 8, 2022, from https://
     sitn.hms.harvard.edu/flash/2017/history-artificial-intelligence/

12.  How AI Boosts Industry Profits and Innovation. (2016,
     September 28). https://www.accenture.com. https://www.
     accenture.com/us-en/insights/artificial-intelligence-summary-
     index

13.  nytimes.com. (2020, January 24). Retrieved March 9, 2022,
     from https://www.nytimes.com/2020/01/24/business/london-
     police-facial-recognition.html

14. Mobile Fact Sheet. (2021, April 21). Pew Research Center: Internet, Science & Tech. Retrieved March 9, 2022, from https://www.pewresearch.org/internet/fact-sheet/mobile/

15. News Release | IHS Markit Online Newsroom. (2019, April 10). Fintech Finance. Retrieved May 10, 2022, from https://news.ihsmarkit.com/prviewer/release_only/slug/technology-global-business-value-artificial-intelligence-banking-reach-300-billion-203

16. Schooley, S. (2022, August 26). The Best Background Check Companies of 2022. Business News Daily. Retrieved April 24, 2022, from https://www.businessnewsdaily.com/7638-best-background-check-services.html

17. Protalinski, E. (2012, May 3). 13 million US Facebook users don't change privacy settings. ZDNET. Retrieved April 24, 2022, from https://www.zdnet.com/article/13-million-us-facebook-users-dont-change-privacy-settings/

18. Smith, J. (2013, April 16). How Social Media Can Help (Or Hurt) You In Your Job Search. Forbes. Retrieved April 24, 2022, from https://www.forbes.com/sites/jacquelynsmith/2013/04/16/how-social-media-can-help-or-hurt-your-job-search/?sh=3d5de06b7ae2

19. LibGuides: Machine Learning and AI: Find Datasets. (n.d.). Retrieved April 24, 2022, from https://guides.library.cmu.edu/c.php?g=844845&p=6191907

20. Is Having a Smartphone a Requirement in 2022? (2022, April 5). Investopedia. Retrieved April 24, 2022, from https://www.investopedia.com/is-having-a-smartphone-a-requirement-in-2021-5190186

21. International Telecommunication Union (ITU), 2021). Measuring digital development Facts and figures 2021. Geneva: ITU.

22. Fact Sheet: Department of Commerce's Use of Bipartisan Infrastructure Deal Funding to Help Close the Digital Divide. (2021, November 10). U.S. Department of Commerce. Retrieved April 24, 2022, from https://www.commerce. gov/news/fact-sheets/2021/11/fact-sheet-department-commerces-use-bipartisan-infrastructure-deal-funding

23. Bringing Africa Up to High Speed. (n.d.). Retrieved April 24, 2022, from https://www.ifc.org/wps/wcm/connect/news_ext_content/ifc_external_corporate_site/news+and+events/news/cm-stories/cm-connecting-africa

24. Ice, A. Z. A. L. (2021, January 19). Why computer occupations are behind strong STEM employment growth in the 2019â"29 decade : Beyond the Numbers: U.S. Bureau of Labor Statistics. Retrieved April 24, 2022, from https://www.bls.gov/opub/btn/volume-10/why-computer-occupations-are-behind-strong-stem-employment-growth.htm

25. Goal 9 | Department of Economic and Social Affairs. (n.d.). Retrieved May 24, 2022, from https://sdgs.un.org/goals/goal9

26. Rural Electrification Act (1936). (2020, October 20). Living New Deal. Retrieved May 24, 2022, from https://livingnewdeal.org/glossary/rural-electrification-act-1936/

27. A4AI Alliance For Affordable Internet. (2022, September 8). Home. Alliance for Affordable Internet. Retrieved May 24, 2022, from https://a4ai.org/

28. The Impact of Social Media Usage on Work Efficiency: The Perspectives of Media Synchronicity and Gratifications. (2021,

July 28). Frontiers. Retrieved May 24, 2022, from https://www.frontiersin.org/articles/10.3389/fpsyg.2021.693183/full#:%7E:text=Regarding%20the%20relationship%20between%20social,Leftheriotis%20and%20Giannakos%2C%202014)

29. Front. Psychol., 28 July 2021
Sec. Organizational Psychology
https://doi.org/10.3389/fpsyg.2021.693183

30. Be careful before you stream: Safe practices for live-streaming your.. (n.d.). Retrieved May 24, 2022, from https://us.norton.com/blog/kids-safety/safe-practices-for-live-streaming-your-gaming

31. Best Ad Blocker & Privacy Browser. (n.d.). Ghostery. Retrieved May 24, 2022, from https://www.ghostery.com

32. CookiePro. (2021, October 18). What is a Tracking Cookie? - Knowledge. Retrieved February 24, 2022, from https://www.cookiepro.com/knowledge/tracking-cookie/#:%7E:text=A%20tracking%20cookie%20is%20a,%2C%20purchase%20trends%2C%20and%20more

33. Usage Statistics of Cookies for Websites, February 2022. (n.d.). Retrieved March 24, 2022, from https://w3techs.com/technologies/details/ce-cookies

34. Kaspersky. (2022, April 18). What is an IP Address – Definition and Explanation. www.kaspersky.com. Retrieved March 26, 2022, from https://www.kaspersky.com/resource-center/definitions/what-is-an-ip-address

35. Temkin, D. (2021, March 3). Charting a course towards a more privacy-first web. Google. Retrieved April 26, 2022, from https://blog.google/products/ads-commerce/a-more-privacy-first-web/

36. Bogna, J. (2021, November 19). Privacy vs. Security: What's the Difference? How-To Geek. Retrieved May 26, 2022, from https://www.howtogeek.com/765272/privacy-vs-security-whats-the-difference/#:%7E:text=Privacy%20refers%20to%20the%20control,protected%20your%20personal%20information%20is

37. Technology Networks. (2020, April 27). A Privacy Paradox: Why Do People So Readily Give Up Information Online? Informatics From Technology Networks. Retrieved June 26, 2022, from https://www.technologynetworks.com/informatics/news/a-privacy-paradox-why-do-people-so-readily-give-up-information-online-333948

38. WhoTracks.me - Bringing Transparency to Online Tracking. (n.d.). Retrieved June 26, 2022, from https://whotracks.me/

39. What Data Is Collected About You - Blog. (2020, October 27). GlobalSign. Retrieved March 26, 2022, from https://www.globalsign.com/en/blog/what-data-is-collected-about-you-online#:%7E:text=When%20browsing%20the%20internet%2C%20you,the%20tip%20of%20the%20iceberg%E2%80%A6

40. Hafiz Burhan Ul Haqi, et al. (2020). The Impact Of Social Media: A Survey. Lahore: INTERNATIONAL JOURNAL OF SCIENTIFIC & TECHNOLOGY RESEARCH.

41. Auxier, B. (2020, October 15). 64% of Americans say social media have a mostly negative effect on the way things are going in the U.S. today. Pew Research Center. Retrieved March 26, 2022, from https://www.pewresearch.org/fact-tank/2020/10/15/64-of-americans-say-social-media-have-a-mostly-negative-effect-on-the-way-things-are-going-in-the-u-s-today/

42. Shewan, D. (2022, September 24). The Comprehensive Guide to Online Advertising Costs. WordStream. Retrieved April 26, 2022, from https://www.wordstream.com/blog/ws/2017/07/05/online-advertising-costs

43. Jeff Wilke, former CEO of Amazon Worldwide Consumer. (2019, June 5). A drone program taking flight. US About Amazon. https://www.aboutamazon.com/news/transportation/a-drone-program-taking-flight

44. Mobile Fact Sheet. (2021, November 23). Pew Research Center: Internet, Science & Tech. Retrieved April 26, 2022, from https://www.pewresearch.org/internet/fact-sheet/mobile/

45. Jenkings, R. (2012, April 4). How much is your email address worth? The Drum. Retrieved March 26, 2022, from https://www.thedrum.com/opinion/2012/04/04/how-much-your-email-address-worth

46. Harrison, S. (n.d.). Can you make money selling your data? BBC Worklife. Retrieved June 26, 2022, from https://www.bbc.com/worklife/article/20180921-can-you-make-money-selling-your-data

47. How Much is Your Data Worth? The Complete Breakdown for 2021. (2021, July 13). Retrieved April 26, 2022, from https://www.invisibly.com/learn-blog/how-much-is-data-worth

48. Youtube [TEDx Talks]. (2018, November 1). Owning Your Digital Self: Monetizing Your Personal Data | Dana Budzyn | TEDxPasadena. YouTube. Retrieved June 16, 2022, from https://www.youtube.com/watch?v=H27PdSnusCQ

49. Honeygain - Make Money From Home. (n.d.). Retrieved June 16, 2022, from https://r.honeygain.me/wallethacks

50. Datacoup. (n.d.). Reclaim Your Personal Data. Retrieved June 16, 2022, from https://datacoup.com/

51. Deep, A. (2021, December 9). How AI Is Transforming The Future Of Healthcare Industry. Medium. Retrieved April 10, 2022, from https://medium.com/hackernoon/how-ai-is-transforming-the-future-of-healthcare-industry-f6020cc18323

52. Capgemini. (2018, December 17). Retail superstars: How unleashing AI across functions offers a multi-billion dollar opportunity. Retrieved June 10, 2022, from https://www.capgemini.com/news/press-releases/ai-in-retail-report/

53. Statista. (2022, May 16). Number of global social network users 2018-2027. Retrieved May 22, 2022, from https://www.statista.com/statistics/278414/number-of-worldwide-social-network-users/

54. ProPublica. (2016, December 27). Facebook Doesn't Tell Users Everything It Really Knows About Them. https://www.propublica.org/article/facebook-doesnt-tell-users-everything-it-really-knows-about-them

55. Social Network Usage & Growth Statistics: How Many People Use Social Media in 2022? (2021, October 10). https://backlinko.com/. https://backlinko.com/social-media-users

56. CareerBuilder Hiring Solutions. (2018, August 9). More Than Half of Employers Have Found Content on Social Media That Caused Them NOT to Hire a Candidate, According to Recent CareerBuilder Survey. Press Room | Career Builder. https://press.careerbuilder.com/2018-08-09-More-Than-Half-of-Employers-Have-Found-Content-on-Social-Media-That-Caused-Them-NOT-to-Hire-a-Candidate-According-to-Recent-Career-Builder-Survey

57. Weissberger, A. (2022, February 20). Credit Suisse: Metaverse to push data usage by 20 times worldwide by 2032. Technology Blog. https://techblog.comsoc.org/2022/02/20/credit-suisse-metaverse-to-push-data-usage-by-20-times-worldwide-by-2032/

58. Mileva, G. (2022, April 25). 20 Brands Leaping into the Metaverse. Influencer Marketing Hub. Retrieved May 1, 2022, from https://influencermarketinghub.com/metaverse-brands/#toc-9

59. Gibson, D. (2022, January 17). 5 brands already boldly embracing the metaverse. The Drum. Retrieved May 1, 2022, from https://www.thedrum.com/news/2022/01/17/5-brands-already-boldly-embracing-the-metaverse

60. Ernest, M. (2021, December 3). Want to wear Balenciaga in the metaverse? The brand is making it happen. Input. Retrieved June 1, 2022, from

61. adidas. (n.d.). Retrieved June 1, 2022, from https://www.adidas.com/into_the_metaverse

62. O'Neill, S. (n.d.). The Future of Data in the Metaverse. Retrieved June 1, 2022, from https://www.lxahub.com/stories/the-future-of-data-in-the-metaverse

63. Ma, A. (2022, May 23). What is the metaverse, and what can we do there? The Conversation. Retrieved June 1, 2022, from https://theconversation.com/what-is-the-metaverse-and-what-can-we-do-there-179200

64. Users – Tor Metrics. (n.d.). Retrieved May 28, 2022, from https://metrics.torproject.org/userstats-relay-country.html

# With Appreciation

If you enjoyed reading this book, help us spread the word and also leave your feedback at ReclaimYourDigitalGold.com

Or visit Amazon Kindle Direct Publishing (KDP) and leave a review.

https://amazon.com/review/create-review?&asin=B0BP97CLDK

Also connect with author at Wayne@TruthCommunications.org

Instagram.com/hinds.wayne
IG DM @Hinds.Wayne

Facebook.com/whinds
FB DM @WHinds